THE COMPLETE GUIDE TO STARTING AN AIRBNB BUSINESS

ABOUT AUTHOR

Welcome to the author page of Jason Westlund, the creative mind behind "The Complete Guide to Starting an Airbnb Business." With a passion for hospitality and a wealth of experience in the short-term rental industry, Jason is eager to share his knowledge and perspectives with aspiring Airbnb hosts.

As a seasoned Airbnb host, Jason understands the challenges and rewards of running a successful Airbnb business. From preparing properties for guests to navigating legal considerations and maximizing profitability, Jason has honed his skills through years of hands-on experience.

In "The Complete Guide to Starting an Airbnb Business," Jason combines his practical knowledge with his passion for helping others succeed. Whether you're a first-time host looking to dip your toes into the world of Airbnb or an experienced host seeking to take your business to the next level, this comprehensive guide has something for everyone.

Through clear and accessible language, Jason demystifies starting and running an Airbnb business. From understanding the Airbnb business model to providing excellent customer service, each chapter is packed with actionable advice, real-life examples, and practical tips to help you succeed in the competitive world of short-term rentals.

But "The Complete Guide to Starting an Airbnb Business" is more than a how-to manual. It's a roadmap to success, filled with encouragement, motivation, and inspiration for aspiring Airbnb hosts. Jason's genuine enthusiasm for Airbnb hosting shines through on every page, reminding readers that with dedication, hard work, and the proper guidance, their Airbnb dreams are within reach.

Beyond the book, Jason is committed to supporting his readers on their Airbnb journey. Whether you have questions, need clarification, or want to share your success stories, Jason is here to help. Connect with him on social media, join his online community of Airbnb hosts, or email him for personalized support and guidance.

In conclusion, "The Complete Guide to Starting an Airbnb Business" is more than just a guidebook—it's your ticket to unlocking the full potential of Airbnb hosting. Let Jason Westlund be your trusted companion on this exciting journey as you embark on becoming a successful Airbnb host.

TABLE OF CONTENTS

INTRODUCTION

Embarking on becoming an Airbnb host is an adventure filled with opportunities, challenges, and immense learning. This guide is crafted from a wealth of personal experience and expertise to share insights and practical wisdom to help you navigate the exciting world of Airbnb hosting. In these pages, you'll uncover a treasure trove of knowledge, ranging from setting up your space to managing and scaling your Airbnb business.

The allure of Airbnb lies in its innovative business model, which has revolutionized the way people travel and stay in places around the world. It offers a unique blend of comfort, local experience, and affordability that traditional hotels often need help to match. By opening your home to travellers, you're earning an income and becoming part of a global community that values connection, sharing, and cultural exchange. However, as with any venture, there are challenges and potential drawbacks. This guide aims to provide a balanced view, helping you confidently navigate them.

Preparing your property for guests is more than just tidying up; it's about creating an inviting and comfortable environment that reflects your taste and local culture. This aspect of Airbnb hosting is both an art and a science, requiring attention to detail and an understanding of what makes a space welcoming and functional. You'll also learn about the legal and safety considerations to ensure your hosting journey is enjoyable and compliant with regulations.

Listing your property on Airbnb is a crucial step. Crafting a compelling property listing is an art in itself, requiring you to showcase your space in a way that attracts potential guests. This guide will offer insights into effective pricing strategies, availability management, and reservation management. We delve into the nuances of guest experience and hospitality, providing tips on offering excellent customer service and creating memorable stays for your guests. Handling guest inquiries and managing reviews are also key aspects of being a successful host, and you'll find practical advice on these topics.

Legal and regulatory considerations must be considered. As an Airbnb host, it's imperative to understand and adhere to local laws, regulations, and taxation requirements. This book will help you navigate these aspects, ensuring your business is profitable and legally sound. Covering insurance for hosts is another critical topic, offering peace of mind and protection for you and your guests.

To draw visitors, marketing and advertising are essential to building a strong online presence. This guide will explore strategies for making your listing stand out, leveraging social media and other marketing channels to reach a wider audience. The chapter on managing your Airbnb business is about the day-to-day aspects of hosting. It covers efficient time management, handling bookings, check-ins, and check-outs, and provides insights into outsourcing tasks when necessary.

For those looking to expand their venture, the chapter on scaling your Airbnb business is invaluable. It covers everything from expanding to multiple properties, hiring staff, and maximizing profitability. Success stories and case studies of other Airbnb hosts offer real-life insights and inspiration, showing what's possible with dedication and smart strategies.

As the Airbnb market evolves, staying abreast of future trends and innovations is crucial. This guide will help you prepare for what lies ahead in the short-term rental industry, ensuring that your business thrives today and remains relevant and successful in the future.

This book is not just a collection of tips and advice; it's a comprehensive guide to building a successful Airbnb business.

It's designed to inspire, educate, and empower you, the aspiring Airbnb host, to create a rewarding and sustainable venture. Through this journey, you'll achieve financial success and become part of a vibrant community of hosts who make the world a little smaller, one stay at a time.

Your personal experience and expertise in the field

Diving into the world of Airbnb hosting was a journey that started for me a few years ago, born out of curiosity and a desire to explore new avenues of income. It all began with the quaint little apartment I owned in the heart of the city, which I realized had more potential than just being my home. The decision to transform it into an Airbnb space wasn't just a financial one; it was about creating an experience for myself and the guests I would host.

The first steps were tentative. I remember spending hours researching, reading about other hosts' experiences, and trying to understand what makes an Airbnb space special. The more I learned, the more I realized that hosting isn't just about providing a bed for the night. It's about offering travellers a slice of your world, a home away from home.

My journey was fraught with learning curves. From understanding how to list my property effectively to figuring out the right pricing strategy, each step was a lesson in hospitality and business. I made mistakes, like underestimating the importance of a well-written listing or needing to prepare more for a guest's arrival. But with each guest, I grew more confident and adept at anticipating needs and managing expectations.

One of the most rewarding aspects of being an Airbnb host has been meeting people from all walks of life. I've hosted families on vacation, business travellers, and couples on romantic getaways. Each guest brought a new story and experience, which taught me something new about hosting, different cultures, and myself.

Customer service, I realized, is at the heart of Airbnb hosting. It's not just about providing a clean and comfortable space; it's about being attentive, responsive, and going above and beyond to ensure your visitors have a memorable stay. I learned to be proactive in communication, always ready to offer local tips, and quickly resolve any issues. Positive reviews from guests weren't just gratifying; they were affirmations that I was on the right path.

Navigating the legal and regulatory landscape was another crucial part of my journey. Understanding local laws, obtaining the necessary permits, and setting up the right insurance were essential steps to ensure that my Airbnb venture was successful, compliant, and secure.

As my experience grew, so did my ambition. I started exploring ways to market my listing better, using social media and other online platforms. I experimented with different strategies, learned from what other successful hosts were doing, and adapted their best practices to suit my unique offering.

The most challenging yet exciting part of this journey has been scaling up. Moving from hosting one property to managing multiple listings was a significant leap. It involved not just more investment but also more complex management. I learned about time management, efficient scheduling, and even outsourcing certain tasks to maintain the quality of my offerings.

This journey has not just been about building a successful business; it's been a journey of personal growth. Each step, each decision, and each interaction has shaped me into a more astute business person, a better host, and a more empathetic individual.

In sharing my story, I aim to inspire and guide others embarking on their own Airbnb hosting journey. The road may have its bumps; however, the material and immaterial benefits make the work worthwhile. It's about creating connections, building a business, and being part of a global community redefining travel and hospitality.

What readers can expect to learn from the book

When you pick up this book, you're not just starting to read another guide; you're opening the door to a journey that could transform your home into a welcoming space for travellers and turn your entrepreneurial dreams into reality. This book is a comprehensive guide, meticulously crafted to take you through every step of becoming a successful Airbnb host.

From the initial chapters, you'll gain a deep understanding of what Airbnb is and why it has become such a popular option for travellers and hosts alike. You'll learn about the benefits of being an Airbnb host, which goes beyond the additional income. Hosting offers the chance to meet diverse people, share your culture, and become part of a global community of hosts and travellers. But it's not all rosy; there are challenges and potential drawbacks, too. This book will give you a realistic picture of what to expect and how to navigate these challenges effectively.

As you delve deeper, the book will guide you through preparing your property for guests. This isn't just about cleaning and arranging furniture; it's about creating an environment that guests will love and remember. You'll find detailed advice on creating a comfortable, functional space that reflects your style and the local culture.

Then comes the crucial part of listing your property on Airbnb. This book will take you through creating a compelling property listing - from writing an engaging description to setting the right price. You'll learn to manage your availability and reservations to maximize your earnings and maintain a work-life balance.

Guest experience and hospitality are at the heart of Airbnb hosting; this book covers that extensively. You'll learn to provide excellent customer service, handle guest inquiries, and manage reviews. These abilities are necessary to succeed as a host and ensure guests leave with happy memories.

The legal and regulatory landscape of Airbnb hosting can be complex, but this book simplifies it for you. You'll get a clear understanding of the local laws, tax implications, and insurance requirements. This knowledge is crucial to ensure your hosting journey is smooth and trouble-free.

In today's digital world, marketing and promotion are key to getting your listing noticed. This book will provide you with practical methods for attracting guests, using social media for promotion, and building a strong online presence. These skills are invaluable in making your Airbnb listing stand out in a crowded marketplace.

Managing an Airbnb business requires organization, time management, and, sometimes, the ability to delegate. You'll learn how to handle bookings, check-ins, and check-outs efficiently. For those considering scaling up their business, this book offers insights into managing multiple properties and building a team.

Real-life success stories and case studies of Airbnb hosts are sprinkled throughout the book, offering inspiration and practical lessons. These stories showcase the diversity of the Airbnb community and the different paths to success.

As Airbnb continues to evolve, staying updated with trends and innovations is crucial. This book will give you a glimpse into the future of Airbnb hosting, helping you stay ahead and adapt to changing market dynamics.

This book is more than just a guide; it's a comprehensive resource that will give you the information, abilities, and self-assurance to start and grow your Airbnb business. Whether you're a new host or looking to improve your existing listing, this book has something valuable for everyone. It's your mentor, guiding you through every aspect of Airbnb hosting, helping you avoid common pitfalls, and setting you up for success.

Chapter 1

UNDERSTANDING THE AIRBNB BUSINESS MODEL

Airbnb, a name that has become synonymous with travel and homestays, is a platform that has revolutionized the way people think about accommodation while travelling. It's a concept that intertwines the comfort of home with the excitement of exploring new places. Airbnb allows users to let people rent out their houses or spare rooms to guests, turning ordinary spaces into unique places for travellers.

At its core, Airbnb operates as a two-sided marketplace. On one side, there are hosts - people like you and me, who have space to share, be it a spare room, an apartment, or even a treehouse. These hosts list their spaces on Airbnb, providing descriptions, photos, and the price. On the other side are the travellers looking for places to stay that offer more personality, comfort, and, often, more value than traditional hotels.

What makes Airbnb stand out is its emphasis on authentic and personal experiences. It's not just about finding a place to sleep; it's about discovering homes with character, telling a story, and allowing travellers to live like locals. This is why you might find a cosy apartment in the heart of Paris, a beachside villa in Bali, or a rustic cabin in Colorado, each offering a unique experience that traditional hotels often can't match.

The process of booking a stay on Airbnb is straightforward. Travellers search for spaces in their desired location, filter based on their preferences, check availability and then book their stay. Hosts can review who stays in their homes, and hosts and guests can communicate through the platform to arrange details like check-in times and any special requirements.

Safety and trust are key pillars of Airbnb's model. The platform includes:

- ➤ Verified profiles.

- ➤ A secure messaging system.

- ➤ A review method that enables both hosts and guests to leave feedback about their experiences.

This openness fosters a sense of trust in the community, ensuring that both hosts and guests can feel confident in their transactions.

For hosts, Airbnb offers an opportunity to earn extra income from their property or spare room. But it's more than just a financial transaction. Being an Airbnb host means joining a community of people who enjoy sharing their spaces and connecting with others. Hosts often provide local tips and recommendations, adding a personal touch to their guests' travel experiences.

For travellers, Airbnb opens up a world of possibilities. It offers a more diverse range of accommodation options at various prices, catering to different needs and preferences. From luxurious to budget-friendly, from urban apartments to rural retreats, Airbnb has something for everyone. Plus, staying in an Airbnb can offer a more immersive experience, allowing travellers to live like locals and explore destinations from a unique perspective.

The impact of Airbnb extends beyond individual hosts and travellers. It has influenced the tourism industry, local economies, and even the way cities and towns are experienced by visitors. By providing travellers with more options for accommodation, Airbnb has made travel more accessible and diversified, supporting local businesses and communities along the way.

In summary, Airbnb is more than just a platform for booking accommodation. It's a gateway to new experiences, a bridge between hosts and travellers, and a catalyst for community and connection. Whether you're looking to explore the world from a local's perspective or share your own space with others, Airbnb offers a unique and personal way to travel and connect with people from all over the globe.

The benefits of becoming an Airbnb host

Becoming an Airbnb host opens up a world of opportunities and benefits beyond just earning extra income. It's a journey that transforms your space into a gateway for travellers and offers a unique chance to connect with people from all over the globe.

One of the most obvious advantages of hosting on Airbnb is the financial gain. By renting out a spare room or your entire home, you can tap into a lucrative source of income. This extra money can be a game-changer for many, helping to pay off mortgages, fund home improvements, or even support other hobbies and passions. The beauty of Airbnb is its flexibility; you can decide when to rent out your space and for how much, giving you control over your earnings.

But hosting on Airbnb is about more than just the money. It's also about the rich cultural exchanges when you open your home to guests from diverse backgrounds. As a host, you get the unique opportunity to meet people from different parts of the world, each with their own stories and experiences. These interactions can broaden your horizons, offer new perspectives, and often lead to lasting friendships.

A deep sense of satisfaction comes from playing a part in someone's travel experience. As a host, you provide more than just a place to sleep; you're helping to create memories for your guests. Whether by offering local tips, suggesting the best places to eat, or just being there to chat, you can significantly impact their journey. Many hosts enjoy being ambassadors of their local area, sharing the hidden gems and experiences that only locals know about.

For those with a flair for hospitality, Airbnb hosting allows you to express this passion. It's an opportunity to create a welcoming space where every little detail, from the decor to the comfort of the bed, contributes to your guest's experience. The creativity involved in setting up and managing your Airbnb can be incredibly fulfilling, turning hosting into an enjoyable and rewarding hobby.

Another benefit is the learning and personal growth of being an Airbnb host. It's not just about understanding how to manage a rental; it's about developing skills in communication, customer service, marketing, and even basic maintenance. This journey of learning and growth can boost your confidence and even inspire new career paths or business ventures.

Airbnb hosting also contributes to the local economy. By attracting travellers, you indirectly support local businesses, whether the cafe down the street or the local tour guide. This helps bolster the community and fosters a sense of pride in showcasing what your area has to offer.

In today's digital age, Airbnb also offers the opportunity to build a strong online presence. You can develop a personal brand through your listing, reviews, and interactions with guests. This can be particularly beneficial if you're looking to expand into other areas of hospitality or tourism.

Lastly, Airbnb hosting offers flexibility that few other side hustles can. You have complete control over when you host, how often, and the rules for your space. This flexibility means you can tailor your hosting around your lifestyle, making it an ideal option for people from all walks of life, whether you're a busy professional, a stay-at-home parent, or a retiree.

Being an Airbnb host is a multifaceted experience that offers much more than just additional income. It's about cultural exchange, personal satisfaction, community building, and personal growth. For those willing to put in the effort, the rewards of Airbnb hosting can be far-reaching, touching not just your life but also the lives of your guests and your community.

Potential drawbacks and challenges

While becoming an Airbnb host offers many rewards, it is critical to recognize that many difficulties and potential drawbacks are involved. Knowing these things is essential for anyone considering the world of Airbnb hosting, as it prepares you for the realities of what to expect and how to handle them best.

One of the first challenges you might encounter is the initial investment and the ongoing maintenance costs. Preparing your space for guests often requires more than just a quick clean-up. You should invest in quality furniture, bedding, and other amenities to ensure your guests' comfort. Additionally, the wear and tear from hosting multiple guests can lead to more frequent repairs and maintenance, adding to your ongoing costs.

Then there's the matter of time and effort involved. Managing an Airbnb listing is a collaborative task. It requires active involvement - from keeping the calendar updated and communicating with potential and current guests to cleaning and preparing your space for new arrivals. This can be particularly demanding if you have a full-time job or other commitments.

Another potential drawback is the inconsistency of income. Unlike a traditional rental, Airbnb income can fluctuate based on season, local events, and competition. There might be times when your space is booked back-to-back and others when it sits empty. This uncertainty can be difficult, particularly if you depend on this income to cover significant expenses.

Handling guest-related issues is another aspect that can be challenging. Not all guests will respect your space or abide by the house rules. You might encounter property damage, noise complaints, or other conflicts. While not the norm, these incidents can be stressful and require tactful and swift resolution.

There's also the challenge of achieving and maintaining high ratings and positive reviews. In the Airbnb world, your reputation is everything. A couple of negative reviews can significantly impact your ability to attract new guests. This pressure to consistently provide outstanding service and maintain a pristine space can be demanding.

Keeping up with the legal and regulatory environment can be another hurdle. The rules surrounding short-term rentals vary greatly from place to place and can change frequently. Keeping abreast of these regulations, acquiring the necessary permits, and paying the appropriate taxes can be complex and time-consuming.

For those living in the property they're hosting, there's a loss of privacy to consider. Having strangers in your home can feel intrusive, and it's not for everyone. Balancing your personal life while being available and accommodating to your guests can sometimes be delicate.

Finally, there's the impact on your neighbours and community. Only some people are enthusiastic about having short-term rentals in their neighbourhood. Issues like increased noise, parking challenges, and a changing community dynamic can sometimes lead to friction with neighbours.

While Airbnb hosting can be rewarding and profitable, it's important to go into it with open eyes. Understanding the potential drawbacks and challenges helps you prepare and strategize how to address them best. This involves setting realistic expectations, being prepared for financial and time commitments, developing strong communication and problem-solving skills, and staying informed about the legal aspects of hosting. With the right approach, these challenges can be managed, allowing you to enjoy the many benefits of being an Airbnb host.

Chapter 2

SETTING UP YOUR AIRBNB SPACE

Preparing your property for Airbnb guests is crucial in your hosting journey. It's about creating a comfortable, functional, welcoming, and memorable space. The goal is to provide an experience that makes guests feel at home while giving them a taste of something special and unique to your place.

First and foremost, cleanliness is paramount. This goes beyond the regular dusting and vacuuming. You need to ensure that every nook and cranny is spotless. This includes deep cleaning areas like the bathroom and kitchen, where hygiene is critical. Remember, guests have high standards, and their reviews will reflect their experience of your home's cleanliness.

Next, think about the comfort and amenities you provide. This starts with the basics, like a comfortable bed with quality linens, enough pillows, and blankets. Ensure the bathroom is well stocked with fresh towels, toiletries, and extra touches like hand creams or bath salts. In the kitchen, make sure all appliances are in good working order and consider providing essentials like coffee, tea, and basic cooking ingredients. These small additions can make a big difference in the guest's experience.

Creating a welcoming atmosphere is also key. This can be achieved through thoughtful decor and personal touches. Consider the style and theme of your home – is it modern, rustic, or perhaps eclectic? Let your space reflect that. Artwork on the walls, a selection of books, or a guide to your favourite local spots can add character to your space. However, it's important to strike a balance – the space should feel personalized but not overly so. Guests should be able to make it their own during their stay.

Safety and functionality are also important. Ensure all safety devices, like smoke detectors and fire extinguishers, are in place and working. Check that all locks function for the guests' safety and your peace of mind. Wi-Fi is almost a given in today's connected world, so ensure your internet connection is strong and reliable. Leave clear instructions for anything tricky, like a smart TV or a complicated shower system.

It's also wise to anticipate your guests' needs. Think about the small things that could make their stay more comfortable. This could include providing a hairdryer, an iron, extra charging cables, or a list of nearby attractions and recommended restaurants. Consider things like a high chair or a crib if you're hosting families. A cosy chair and a compact workstation can be a thoughtful addition for business travellers.

Another aspect to consider is the outdoor space, if you have one. A tidy, inviting garden, balcony, or patio can be a huge selling point. Simple additions like outdoor seating or a small herb garden can enhance the guest's experience.

Lastly, communication is key. Leave a welcome note with essential information like Wi-Fi passwords, emergency contact numbers, and house rules. Consider creating a guidebook that includes instructions for appliances, recommendations for local eateries, and tips on getting around the area.

Preparing your property for Airbnb guests is about more than just providing a place to sleep. It's about offering an experience that is comfortable, safe, and unique. It calls for close attention to detail, a thorough comprehension of your guests' needs, and a desire to create a memorable stay. With the right preparation, your property can become a sought-after destination for travellers and a source of pride and income for you as a host.

Creating an inviting and comfortable environment

Establishing a warm and welcoming space for your Airbnb guests is an art that ensures they have a memorable stay. It's about crafting a space that doesn't just feel like a place to sleep but where Visitors can unwind, feel at home, and relax.

The first step in this process is to think about the overall ambience of your space. Consider the lighting - soft, warm lights create a cosy and welcoming atmosphere, much more so than harsh, bright lights. Think about adding lamps or even fairy lights for a touch of whimsy and warmth. Natural light also plays a crucial role, so let in as much as possible. Open curtains or blinds instantly make a room feel more spacious and lively.

Next, focus on the furniture. Comfort is key here. Ensure that the sofa is plush and inviting, the chairs are comfortable, and the bed is something you'd want to sleep in yourself. Remember, a good night's sleep can highlight a guest's stay. Invest in a high-quality mattress, cosy blankets, and pillows that offer support and comfort.

The choice of decor can significantly influence the feel of your space. You want your place to have character, but maintaining enough neutrality to appeal to a broad range of tastes is essential. Opt for calming colours and simple patterns. Adding plants is a wonderful way to bring life into a room; they beautify the space and improve air quality. Artwork can also add personality to your space. Select items that honour the area's culture or your style, but avoid anything too polarizing.

Personal touches can make a huge difference. Think about providing a personalized message for your visitors and a small welcome gift like a basket of local snacks or a bottle of wine. This shows thoughtfulness and care that guests will appreciate and remember.

Cleanliness and organization are non-negotiable. Ensure everything is spotless and neatly arranged. Clutter can be overwhelming and uncomfortable, so ensure enough storage space for guests to keep their belongings. This includes ample hangers in the closet, empty drawers, and a small space where guests can work or write.

In terms of amenities, it's the little things that count. Providing basics like toiletries, extra towels, and Wi-Fi is expected. But going the extra mile with things like a coffee maker complete with coffee pods, a selection of teas, or even a guidebook with your personal recommendations for the area can significantly elevate a guest's experience.

If your space allows, create different zones - a place to sleep, a place to eat, and a place to relax. This can be achieved in a small area with smart furniture choices and layout. For instance, a small rug can define the living area, while a foldable dining table can save space yet provide a comfortable eating area.

Remember, creating an inviting space is not just about the physical aspects; it's also about the atmosphere you create. This extends to your interactions with guests. Being warm, accessible, and responsive goes a long way in making guests feel welcome and taken care of.

Creating an inviting and comfortable environment in your Airbnb is about blending aesthetics with functionality. It's about paying attention to details and anticipating your guests' needs. By putting in this effort, you're not just offering a place to stay but an experience that your guests will cherish and remember. And that's what truly makes a successful Airbnb host.

Legal and safety considerations

When you decide to become an Airbnb host, it's not just about creating a welcoming space for guests; it's also crucial to consider the legal and safety aspects of hosting. These considerations are essential to ensure your venture into Airbnb hosting is secure, responsible, and compliant with the law.

Recognizing and abiding by local rules and ordinances should be your first step. The rules for short-term rentals can vary significantly from one place to another. In some cities, you might need to register or obtain a license to host on Airbnb. There could be zoning laws that restrict the use of your property for short-term rentals or specific regulations about the number of days you can host in a year. Researching and understanding these laws is imperative to avoid any legal complications. Sometimes, you might need to inform your homeowners' association or landlord about your intention to host, as they may have rules.

Insurance is another critical aspect. While Airbnb provides a Host Guarantee and Host Protection Insurance, these might only cover some situations. It's wise to review your existing homeowner's or renter's insurance policy to see what's covered and what's not when it comes to hosting guests. In many cases, getting additional insurance that specifically covers short-term rentals is a good idea. This protects you against potential liabilities, such as incidents or injuries that might happen on your land.

Safety for both you and your guests is paramount. This starts with ensuring that your property meets all safety standards. Install detectors for carbon monoxide and smoke in key areas, and ensure that your fire extinguisher is easily accessible and that your first aid kit is well-stocked and up to date. It's also important to perform regular maintenance checks on appliances and electrical systems to prevent hazards.

Providing clear safety information to your guests is equally important. This includes instructions on how to use appliances safely, guidelines for emergencies, and information about local emergency services. Having a well-detailed house manual can be very helpful. This manual includes a clear map of emergency exits and instructions for shutting off gas, electricity, and water in emergencies.

Privacy is another aspect to consider. While you should keep an eye on your property, respecting your guests' privacy is essential. Any surveillance devices, even those outside the property, should be disclosed in your listing. Having surveillance devices in private areas like bedrooms and bathrooms is illegal, and violating this can lead to serious repercussions.

Handling guest data responsibly is also a part of your legal obligations. Be mindful of the information you collect and store from your guests. Ensure that it's kept securely and only for as long as necessary.

The legal and safety aspects of Airbnb hosting require careful consideration and ongoing attention. Staying informed about local laws and regulations, ensuring adequate insurance coverage, maintaining high safety standards, respecting guests' privacy, and handling guest data responsibly are all critical to running a successful and compliant Airbnb business. By taking these aspects seriously, you protect yourself and provide a safe and secure experience for your guests, which is a cornerstone of being a good host.

Chapter 3

LISTING YOUR PROPERTY ON AIRBNB

Creating a compelling property listing for Airbnb is much like telling a story. It's about presenting your space in a way that showcases its features and amenities and captures its unique character and the experience it offers. This is your opportunity to make a great first impression and attract potential guests.

The first thing to focus on is your listing title. This is like the headline of a news article - it needs to be catchy and descriptive, giving potential guests a glimpse of what makes your space special. Use descriptive and appealing words, but avoid exaggerating or misleading information. For example, a title like "Cozy Cottage by the Lake with Spectacular Sunset Views" instantly paints a picture and sets expectations.

Photos are the most critical part of your listing. They will catch a potential guest's eye and encourage them to learn more about your space. High-quality, well-lit photos are a must. Show off each room, but also include details that make your space unique - a close-up of the coffee nook you've set up, the view from the bedroom window, or the collection of books guests can peruse. Consider hiring a professional photographer. Remember, photos are not just about showing the space but about selling a potential experience.

Your description is where you can dive into what makes your space unique. Start with the basics, covering all the amenities and features, then go further. Share what makes your place special. Is it the history of the building, the stunning view from the balcony, or the ultra-comfortable memory foam mattress? Be honest and clear about what guests can expect - if there's no TV, say so, but highlight the selection of board games or books available instead.

Remember to highlight your location. What's nearby? Are there cute cafes, great hiking trails, or a famous museum? This information helps guests picture themselves in your space and neighbourhood, making your listing more appealing. If you're in a quieter, more remote location, highlight the benefits of this - the peace, the nature, the escape from the hustle and bustle.

Pricing your rental is a delicate balance. It's important to research what similar properties in your area are charging. Pricing too high can deter guests, while pricing too low can undervalue your space. Consider what's special about your space that might justify a higher price or what extras you offer - like free parking or a welcome basket.

Managing availability and reservations is also crucial. Ensure your calendar is always up-to-date to avoid double bookings or having to cancel on guests, which can negatively impact your ratings. Set clear check-in and check-out times, and consider offering flexibility where you can - guests often appreciate this.

Finally, reviews are incredibly important. Please encourage your guests to leave a review after their stay, and always respond to positive and negative reviews. This shows potential guests that you value feedback and are committed to providing a great experience.

Creating a compelling Airbnb property listing is about more than just listing the features of your space. It's about crafting a narrative that draws potential guests in, making them feel like they could see themselves enjoying your space. It combines visuals, engaging descriptions, strategic pricing, and good management practices. With attention to detail and creativity, your listing can stand out and attract guests looking for just what you have to offer.

Pricing your rental

Pricing your rental on Airbnb is a crucial aspect of your hosting journey. It's a balancing act where you must consider various factors to set a price that attracts guests while ensuring you get fair compensation for your space and efforts.

The first step in determining the right price is understanding your local market. Look at other listings in your area, especially those similar to yours in size, location, and amenities. This gives you a baseline to understand the going rates. Remember that prices can fluctuate based on season, local events, and even the day of the week. A downtown apartment might fetch a higher price during a big concert or sports event, while a beach house could be more in demand during the summer.

Another factor to consider is the unique qualities of your rental. What sets your place apart? You may have a stunning view, a hot tub, or your place is steeped in history. These features can justify a higher price. However, it's crucial to be realistic. Overpricing can lead to fewer bookings, while underpricing might mean more bookings but less profit and potentially attracting guests who may not value your space.

It's also important to factor in your costs. Calculate the expenses of maintaining your Airbnb – cleaning, supplies, utilities, taxes, and other overheads. Your pricing should cover these costs and also leave room for profit. This ensures that your Airbnb venture is financially sustainable in the long run.

When setting your price, consider starting a little lower to attract your first few guests and gain those all-important initial reviews.

Reviews are gold in the Airbnb world; they build your reputation and can justify higher prices in the future. As you make more money, you can progressively raise your prices for positive reviews and become a more established host.

Another strategy is to be flexible with your pricing. Consider offering discounts for longer stays, attracting guests looking for a longer vacation or a work trip. This fills up your calendar and reduces the work involved in frequent turnovers.

Dynamic pricing is another aspect to consider. Tools that adjust your rental price based on demand, local events, and other market factors are available. These tools can help you maximize your income by automatically adjusting prices for peak times and lowering them when demand is lower, ensuring your space remains competitive.

Communication with guests about your pricing is also important. Be transparent about what they are paying for. If there are extra charges, like a cleaning fee or an additional guest fee, make these clear in your listing. Surprises when it comes to costs can lead to negative reviews.

Lastly, remember to review and adjust your prices regularly. The market can change, new competitors can enter the scene, or your circumstances might evolve. Regularly updating your pricing strategy ensures that you remain competitive and profitable.

Pricing your rental on Airbnb is not a set-it-and-forget-it deal. It requires research, understanding of your local market, consideration of your unique offering, and regular adjustments. By taking a thoughtful approach to pricing, you can create a win-win situation where your guests feel they're getting good value, and you are rewarded fairly for your hosting efforts.

Managing availability and reservations

Managing availability and reservations effectively is critical to being a successful Airbnb host. It involves more than just keeping an updated calendar; it's about strategically planning your hosting schedule, anticipating your guests' needs, and ensuring a smooth experience for both you and them.

One of the first things to consider is how often you want to host. You can make your space available all year round or only during certain seasons or specific days. This decision might depend on your schedule, local demand, or even when your space is at its best – like a beach house in summer or a cosy cabin during the ski season.

Once you've decided when to host, keeping your calendar up to date is crucial. An accurate calendar helps avoid double bookings and affects your search ranking on Airbnb. Regularly updating your availability, blocking out dates when you're not hosting, and promptly confirming reservations help maintain a reliable profile.

Being responsive to reservation requests is equally important. Quick responses show potential guests that you are attentive and considerate, which can be a factor in choosing your place over another. Setting up instant booking can be a great way to attract guests looking for a place on short notice, but make sure you're comfortable with having less control over who books your space.

It's also important to set clear rules and expectations around reservations. This includes check-in and check-out times, cancellation policy, and house rules. Clear communication of these policies from the start helps prevent misunderstandings and ensures a smooth experience for you and your guests.

Sometimes, you may encounter situations where you need to cancel a reservation. While this should be avoided as much as possible due to its impact on your reputation and potential penalties from Airbnb, there are times when it might be unavoidable. In such cases, communicate with your guests as early and empathetically as possible. Offer to help them find alternative accommodations and explain the situation honestly.

Managing guest expectations is another key aspect. Your listing should accurately reflect what guests can expect. This includes details about the space, amenities, and any unique quirks your home might have. Being upfront about potential drawbacks, like a steep staircase or no parking space, can help manage expectations and reduce the risk of guest dissatisfaction.

Another tip for managing reservations effectively is to prepare for turnover. This means having a system for cleaning and resetting your space between guests. Whether you do it yourself or hire a cleaning service, having a checklist ensures that everything is noticed and your space is always ready for the next guest.

Finally, consider the guest experience throughout their stay. This means being available to answer questions, solve problems, and provide local tips. Your interaction with guests doesn't just end with handing over the keys; it's about being a helpful and available host throughout their stay.

Managing availability and reservations on Airbnb needs thorough preparation, close attention to detail, and initiative communication. By staying organized, being responsive, and setting clear expectations, you can manage your bookings effectively, leading to a better experience for you and your guests. This enhances your credibility as a trustworthy host and contributes to your Airbnb venture's success.

Chapter 4

GUEST EXPERIENCE AND HOSPITALITY

Offering top-notch customer support is the foundation of being a successful Airbnb host. It's about creating an experience that leaves your guests feeling valued and cared for, which, in turn, often leads to glowing reviews and repeat bookings. This aspect of hosting extends far beyond just offering a clean and comfortable space.

The journey of providing excellent service begins when a potential guest contacts you. Responding promptly and professionally to inquiries and reservation requests sets the tone for your interactions. Clear and friendly communication helps build trust and reassurance, especially for guests who may be new to Airbnb or travel to your area for the first time.

Once a booking is confirmed, providing guests with detailed information about your space, directions, check-in procedures, and local recommendations can greatly enhance their experience. This shows that you're organized and thoughtful and helps guests feel more prepared and excited about their stay.

Making the process as smooth and welcoming as possible is key during check-in. If you're meeting guests in person, a friendly greeting and a quick tour of the space can make a big difference. Clear instructions and a welcome note can be just as effective for those using self-check-in. Remember, first impressions matter a great deal.

However, the real essence of excellent customer service lies in the small details and gestures that show guests you care about their comfort and experience. This could be as simple as providing extra blankets, a small basket of snacks, or a list of your favourite local cafes and restaurants. Considering your guests' requirements in advance and going above and beyond to meet them can make a stay from ordinary to unforgettable.

Being available and responsive during your guests' stay is also crucial. Guests should feel they can easily reach you if they have questions or if any issues arise. Whether it's a request for more towels, a question about the Wi-Fi password, or dealing with an unexpected maintenance issue, prompt and helpful responses show guests that their comfort is your priority.

It's also important to seek and be open to feedback. Encourage your guests to let you know if anything could improve their stay. This allows you to rectify any issues in real-time and provides valuable insights that can help you improve your space and service for future guests.

After the stay, following up with a thank you message and inviting guests to leave a review demonstrates your commitment to guest satisfaction. Providing excellent service also addresses favourable and unfavourable evaluations graciously and professionally. It shows that you value guest feedback and are committed to continually improving your hosting experience.

Remember, providing excellent customer service in the Airbnb context is not just about transactions; it's about building relationships. Guests are more likely to remember how you made them feel during their stay than the décor of your space or the amenities you provided. They're looking for a comfortable, welcoming, and memorable experience, and you can deliver that as a host.

Excellent customer service as an Airbnb host involves being attentive and responsive and going above and beyond to ensure your guests have a wonderful stay. It's about making them feel welcomed, cared for, and valued. By focusing on these aspects, you enhance your guests' experience and set the foundation for a successful and rewarding hosting journey.

Tips for hosting guests

Hosting guests on Airbnb is an art that combines hospitality, attention to detail, and a genuine desire to provide a memorable experience. Whether you're new to hosting or looking to enhance your skills, here are some tips to help you become a standout Airbnb host.

Firstly, getting to know your guests before they arrive can be invaluable. When a guest books your space, take the time to read their profile and previous reviews. This can give you an insight into their preferences and expectations. A brief exchange through Airbnb's messaging system about their arrival time, reason for travel, and any special requirements they might have shows that you're attentive and care about their experience.

Creating a welcoming environment is crucial. This goes beyond just a clean and tidy space. Think about adding personal touches like a small note welcoming them by name, a local treat, or a vase of fresh flowers. These gestures make guests feel special and valued.

Understanding and respecting your guests' privacy is key. While some guests might enjoy a chat and appreciate local tips from their host, others might prefer minimal interaction. Being able to gauge this and adapt your approach is a sign of a great host.

Clear instructions and information about your space can greatly enhance guests' experience. A well-organized welcome book or guide that includes Wi-Fi passwords, appliance instructions, local emergency numbers, and recommendations for dining and activities can be incredibly helpful. Also, include any house rules or expectations to avoid any misunderstandings.

Anticipating your guests' needs can set you apart as a host. Stocking the bathroom with essentials like shampoo, conditioner, soap, and plenty of toilet paper is necessary. In the kitchen, basics like coffee, tea, sugar, and snacks can be a lifesaver for guests who've had a long journey. If you host families, having board games, books, or a crib can make a big difference.

Maintaining your space is non-negotiable. Regular checks and maintenance ensure that everything is in working order and that any wear and tear are addressed promptly. This keeps your space attractive and functional and prevents any issues during your guests' stay.

Being responsive and available during your guests' stay is important. Guests should feel they can easily contact you if they have questions or if something needs to be fixed. Whether it's a quick response to a message or being on hand to fix an issue, your availability can greatly impact their overall experience.

Asking for feedback at the end of their stay shows that they're committed to improving. It also allows guests to mention anything they might not have brought up during their stay. This may offer insightful information to enhance your space and service.

Finally, saying goodbye and thanking your guests for their stay adds a personal touch that can leave a lasting impression. A simple message wishing them a safe journey and expressing appreciation for choosing your space can make guests feel valued and increase the likelihood of them leaving a positive review.

Hosting guests on Airbnb is about creating a comfortable, welcoming, and memorable experience. It's about being attentive, proactive, and responsive to your guests' needs and expectations. By focusing on these aspects, you ensure your guests have a pleasant stay and lay the groundwork for becoming a highly rated and successful Airbnb host.

Dealing with guest inquiries and reviews

Dealing with guest inquiries and reviews is crucial to the Airbnb hosting experience. It's where communication skills and the ability to manage positive and negative feedback come into play. How you handle these aspects can significantly impact your reputation as a host and the success of your listing.

When it comes to guest inquiries, promptness and clarity are key. Guests often ask questions about your space, availability, or amenities before they book. Responding quickly to these inquiries increases the likelihood of securing a booking and sets a positive tone for your interaction with potential guests. It's important to answer their questions thoroughly and clearly. For example, if a guest asks about parking, provide detailed information about the parking situation, including any costs or restrictions. This helps them plan their trip better and shows that you're a considerate and helpful host.

Equally important is maintaining this level of responsiveness throughout their stay. Guests might have questions or need assistance during their visit. Being accessible and willing to help, whether addressing a Wi-Fi issue or recommending a local restaurant, enhances their experience and your reputation as a caring host.

Now, let's talk about reviews. Reviews are the lifeblood of your Airbnb profile. They provide social proof to potential guests about the quality of your space and your abilities as a host. When you receive positive reviews, make it a point to respond to them. A simple thank you for acknowledging the guest's comments shows your appreciation and engagement with your guests. This can make your listing more attractive to future guests.

However, Handling negative reviews can be more challenging but equally important. If you receive a less-than-favourable review, it's crucial to approach it professionally and constructively. First, take a moment to assess the feedback objectively. Is there any truth to the criticism? Could you have done something differently? Responding to negative reviews calmly and respectfully demonstrates to future guests that you take feedback seriously and are committed to improving your hosting experience. Acknowledge any valid points raised by the guest, apologize if necessary, and explain any steps you're taking to address the issue. This shows that you're responsive and dedicated to providing a great experience.

It's also important to learn from reviews. Guests' favourable and unfavourable comments are invaluable for understanding what you're doing well and what could be improved. Maybe several guests have commented on how comfortable the bed is – a strength you can highlight in your listing. Alternatively, if guests consistently point out that the room is colder than they'd like, it might be time to invest in a better heating solution.

Lastly, encourage guests to leave a review. You can do this in a checkout message, or a thank you note left in the space. Tell them you appreciate their feedback and how it helps you as a host. However, it's important to keep this request polite and non-intrusive.

Dealing with guest inquiries and reviews is essential to being an Airbnb host. It involves being responsive, clear, helpful in your communication, and professional and constructive in handling feedback. By excelling in these areas, you enhance your guests' experience and build a strong, positive reputation on Airbnb, paving the way for ongoing success and satisfaction in your hosting journey.

Chapter 5

LEGAL AND REGULATORY CONSIDERATIONS

It is crucial to comprehend local rules and regulations to be a responsible and successful Airbnb host. It's a task that might seem daunting at first, but it's crucial for ensuring your hosting journey is profitable and compliant with legal standards. Navigating this maze of rules can be like putting together a puzzle – each piece is important and needs to be in the right place for the whole picture to come together.

First and foremost, it's vital to familiarize yourself with the zoning laws in your area. These laws determine whether you can rent your property in the short term. In some cities, there might be specific zones where Airbnb hosting is permitted or limitations on the properties available for rental. It's important to ensure your property falls within the permissible zones and meets any specific criteria set out by the local authorities.

Next, you need to look into licensing and permits. Many cities require hosts to obtain a license or permit to operate a short-term rental. This process might involve filling out applications, paying fees, and passing certain inspections. The requirements can vary greatly from one place to another, so it's essential to check with your local government to understand exactly what's required.

Another crucial aspect is tax compliance. Hosting on Airbnb means you're running a business, and like any business, you need to pay taxes on your earnings. This could include income, sales, or even a specific tourist tax. Some areas have agreements with Airbnb to collect these taxes automatically, but it might be up to you to report and pay them in other places. Maintaining accurate records of your earnings and outlays is key here.

It's also important to be aware of any specific regulations that apply to the running of your Airbnb. This might include rules about noise, waste management, and the number of guests you're allowed to have at one time. These rules are often in place to ensure short-term rentals do not negatively impact the local community.

Sometimes, you may also need to consider the rules of homeowners' associations (HOAs) or condominium boards. These organizations might have restrictions on short-term rentals, ranging from complete bans to specific guidelines you need to follow.

Understanding these laws and regulations might require research and effort, but setting up your Airbnb business is crucial. Ignoring them can lead to fines, legal issues, and even the closure of your listing. It's always better to proactively understand and comply with these rules.

Furthermore, staying updated on these laws and regulations is important as they can change over time. Keeping an eye on local news, joining local host forums, or subscribing to updates from Airbnb or local authorities can help you stay informed.

Recognizing and abiding by local rules and ordinances is fundamental to being an Airbnb host. It involves educating yourself about zoning laws, obtaining necessary licenses and permits, ensuring tax compliance, and adhering to community standards. At the same time, it might seem like a lot of work initially, but getting these elements right is essential for running a legitimate, responsible, and successful Airbnb business. By taking care of these legal and regulatory aspects, you protect yourself and contribute positively to your community and the broader Airbnb ecosystem.

Taxes and permits

Navigating the world of taxes and permits as an Airbnb host can often feel overwhelming, akin to venturing into a complex maze filled with important details and requirements. However, understanding and managing these aspects is crucial for running a successful and legally compliant Airbnb operation.

Firstly, let's talk about permits. Many cities and towns require hosts to obtain authorizations or certifications to legally lease their premises on a short-term basis. This process is like a stamp of approval from your local government, ensuring that your rental meets certain standards and regulations. You must fill out applications, pay fees, and possibly undergo property inspections to obtain these permits. The specifics vary widely depending on your location, so it's important to research the requirements in your area. Some places have straightforward processes, while others may have more stringent requirements. Ignoring these permit requirements can lead to penalties, including fines or suspension of your Airbnb listing, so taking this step seriously is crucial.

Now, onto taxes. As an Airbnb host, you're essentially running a small business, which means you're responsible for reporting and paying taxes on your rental income. This part of hosting can feel like navigating a financial jungle, but it's an unavoidable and important aspect of your responsibilities. You'll likely need to pay income tax on your hosting money. The amount and process for this depend on your country's tax laws and financial situation. Keeping detailed records of your Airbnb income and related expenses is crucial, as you can deduct certain costs, such as cleaning fees, supplies, and a portion of your mortgage or rent, thereby reducing your taxable income.

In addition to income tax, you may also need to handle occupancy, hotel, tourist, or transient occupancy taxes. These taxes are similar to what hotels charge and are typically a percentage of the booking cost paid by the guest. In some areas, Airbnb collects and remits these taxes on behalf of hosts, but in other places, you may be responsible for collecting and paying these taxes yourself. It's important to check Airbnb's policy for your area and understand your obligations.

Staying informed and compliant with tax laws and regulations is more than a one-time task. Tax laws can change, and it's your responsibility to stay current with these changes. Consulting with a tax professional who understands the intricacies of short-term rental taxes can be a wise investment, ensuring you're compliant and taking advantage of any potential tax benefits.

Finally, while dealing with taxes and permits might not be the most exciting part of being an Airbnb host, it's a fundamental component of your business operations. It's about laying a strong, legal foundation for your hosting activities. Taking care of these aspects protects you from hazards associated with the law and finances and adds to the legitimacy and sustainability of the Airbnb community.

Managing taxes and permits as an Airbnb host is critical to your role. It involves understanding and complying with local permit requirements and navigating the complexities of tax obligations. While this can seem daunting initially, approaching it with diligence and seeking professional advice when needed can make this process manageable. By staying informed and compliant, you ensure your Airbnb hosting journey is successful and on the right side of the law.

Insurance for Airbnb hosts

Insurance for Airbnb hosts is a topic that might not be the most exciting part of the hosting journey, but it's undeniably one of the most important. Like a safety net in a trapeze act, the right insurance can give you peace of mind, knowing you're protected against potential risks and unexpected events.

Its regular home insurance might not provide sufficient coverage for Airbnb hosting activities. This is because short-term rentals are generally considered a commercial activity, which is often excluded from standard home insurance policies. Due to this coverage gap, you may be at risk for various risks, from property damage by guests to liability claims if a guest gets injured on your property.

Recognizing this need, Airbnb provides a Host Guarantee and Host Protection Insurance. The Host Guarantee may protect damages to your property caused by guests up to a certain limit. However, it's important to note that this is not an insurance policy and has certain limitations and exclusions. For instance, it may not cover cash, collectables, or damage to shared or communal areas.

The Host Protection Insurance is a liability insurance program that provides primary coverage for Airbnb hosts and landlords if guests get hurt or cause property damage. This can be a crucial protection, as liability claims can be costly and complex. But, like any insurance policy, it has its limitations and terms, which you should understand clearly.

Given these limitations, it's wise to consider purchasing additional insurance specifically designed for short-term rentals. This type of insurance can offer more comprehensive coverage, filling in the gaps left by the Airbnb Host Guarantee and your standard home insurance policy. It can cover scenarios like lost income if damage to your property renders it uninhabitable or more extensive liability coverage in case of guest injuries.

When shopping for insurance, it's crucial to be thorough and clear about your needs—contact insurance providers who understand the Airbnb business model and can offer policies tailored to short-term rental hosts. Discuss your specific situation with them – for instance, if you're hosting in a multi-unit building, your insurance needs might differ from hosting in a standalone house.

Also, consider the type and frequency of your Airbnb hosting. If you rent out your space only occasionally, your insurance needs may differ from someone who hosts frequently or has multiple listings. Be transparent about your hosting activities with your insurance provider to ensure you get the right coverage.

Moreover, it's important to review and update your insurance coverage regularly. As your hosting business grows or changes, so will your insurance needs. Keep an eye on changes in Airbnb's policies or local regulations that might affect your insurance requirements.

Insurance for Airbnb hosts is a critical aspect that shouldn't be overlooked. While Airbnb offers some protection, more is needed to cover the risks associated with short-term rentals fully. Additional insurance specifically designed for Airbnb hosting can provide more comprehensive protection. This ensures that you're complying with Airbnb's requirements and safeguarding your property, finances, and peace of mind. Remember, being well-insured is not just about protecting your assets; it's about ensuring the sustainability and longevity of your Airbnb venture.

Chapter 6

MARKETING AND PROMOTION

Attracting guests to your Airbnb listing is like drawing people into a story. It's about creating an irresistible narrative that captures their imagination and makes them want to be a part of the experience you're offering. In a marketplace as crowded as Airbnb, having strategies to stand out and attract guests is key to the success of your hosting journey.

The cornerstone of attracting guests is your listing itself. It's your primary tool for making that all-important first impression. High-quality, appealing photos are crucial. They should showcase the space and its amenities and convey a sense of warmth and welcome. It's often worth investing in a professional photographer to capture your space in the best light.

Your description also plays a vital role. It should be detailed and honest and highlight what makes your place unique. Whether it's a stunning view, a cosy reading nook, or a collection of board games for family fun, ensure these features are front and centre in your description. Use language that paints a picture and evokes a feeling of staying at your place. However, managing expectations is important by being truthful about what your space offers and its limitations.

Another strategy is to optimize your listing for search. This means using keywords that potential guests are likely to search for. Include these details in your listing if your place is near a famous landmark, a popular event venue, or a sought-after neighbourhood. Regularly updating your listing can also help boost its ranking in search results.

Pricing is another critical factor. It needs to be competitive but also reflects the value of your offering—research similar listings in your area to understand the market rate. Consider offering introductory rates to attract your first guests and build up those all-important reviews.

Speaking of reviews, they are one of your most powerful tools for attracting guests. Encourage every guest to leave a review and always respond to positive and negative reviews in a thoughtful and professional manner. This shows that you value feedback and that you're engaged and attentive as a host.

Creating a unique experience can also set your listing apart. This could be anything from offering a local culinary treat upon arrival to providing custom guides to the city. These personal touches make your space memorable and can lead to word-of-mouth recommendations.

Promoting your listing outside of Airbnb can also be effective. Use social media to share your listing and engage with potential guests. Create posts showcasing your space and the experiences guests can have while staying there. If you have a blog or website, use it to share stories and updates about your hosting experience.

Partnerships can be another avenue to explore. Connect with local businesses, like cafes or tour operators, and see if there's potential for cross-promotion. This enhances the guest experience and broadens your reach to potential guests.

Flexibility in booking and cancellations can also make your listing more attractive. Guests appreciate having some degree of flexibility, especially in uncertain times. A moderate cancellation policy or accommodating check-in and check-out times can make your listing more appealing.

Attracting guests to your Airbnb listing involves a mix of compelling presentation, strategic pricing, excellent service, and unique experiences. It's about creating a listing that stands out in the sea of options and resonates with the kind of guests you're hoping to attract. By focusing on these strategies, you can draw more guests to your space, provide them with memorable stays, and build a successful Airbnb hosting experience.

Using social media and other marketing channels

Using social media and other marketing channels effectively may greatly increase the appeal and visibility of your Airbnb listing. In today's digital age, these platforms are not just tools for connection but powerful avenues to showcase your space and attract guests worldwide.

With its vast and diverse audience, social media is a fantastic place to start. Platforms like Instagram, Facebook, and Pinterest are ideal for visually showcasing your property. Regularly posting high-quality images of your space featuring unique aspects or changes you've made can create an appealing visual story. These posts can be enhanced with engaging captions that share little snippets about what makes your space special, like a recently updated decor, the serene view from the balcony, or the cosy spot where visitors can have coffee.

But it's not just about posting pictures. Engaging with your audience is key. Responding to comments, asking questions, and even sharing behind-the-scenes glimpses into your life as a host can build a connection with potential guests. You could share stories of the local area, tips for travellers, or even testimonials from past guests. This brings your listing to life and helps build trust and interest.

Hashtags are another powerful tool on platforms like Instagram and Twitter. They can increase the reach of your posts, connecting you with people searching for places to stay in your area or those interested in travel and accommodation ideas.

Facebook groups can be an invaluable asset as well. Joining local travel or community groups and participating in discussions can help you get the word out about your Airbnb. Just be sure to follow the group's rules about self-promotion.

Aside from social media, consider other marketing channels. If you have a blog or a website, use it to create content about your hosting experience or the attractions in your local area. This improves the visibility of your listing and positions you as a knowledgeable host passionate about providing a great experience.

Additionally, email marketing is a channel that can be effective, especially if you've been hosting for a while and have a list of past guests. Sending out updates about your property, special offers, or even seasonal greetings can keep you in mind for their next trip. It's a more direct communication method and can help foster repeat bookings.

Collaboration can be beneficial, too. Partnering with local businesses or influencers can increase your reach. For instance, you could offer a local tour guide a free night's stay in exchange for them featuring your property on their platform. This brings your listing to a wider audience and offers an added experience to your guests.

Paid marketing, such as Google AdWords and ads on Facebook, can also be a part of your strategy. These platforms let you focus on particular demographics, like people who have shown interest in travel or those planning a trip to your area. While this involves an investment, it can lead to a higher rate of targeted visibility for your listing.

Using social media and other marketing channels effectively requires a mix of creativity, engagement, and strategic thinking.

It's about showcasing the unique aspects of your property, building connections with potential guests, and staying active and visible in the digital space. By leveraging these platforms, you can attract a wider audience, create interest in your space, and ultimately increase your bookings. This approach promotes your listing and helps build a brand for your Airbnb, making it a go-to option for travellers looking for a place that offers more than just a bed for the night.

Building a strong online presence

Building a strong online presence as an Airbnb host is about creating a digital identity that captures the essence of your offering and connects with potential guests. In a world where online impressions are increasingly influential, establishing a robust online presence is key to attracting guests and growing your Airbnb business.

Starting with your Airbnb listing is your primary online touchpoint. Ensure your listing is complete, detailed, and updated regularly. High-quality photos, a compelling and clear description, and quick responses to inquiries set the foundation for your online presence. But it doesn't stop there.

Expanding your digital footprint beyond the Airbnb platform can significantly enhance your visibility. Creating a dedicated Instagram account or Facebook page for your rental can be a game-changer. You can share lovely pictures of your space, share updates, and connect with potential guests. It's also a space to showcase your property's unique experiences, from a sunny reading nook to breathtaking views from the balcony.

Engagement is key in the social media realm. Frequently publishing material, answering messages and comments, and interacting with your followers help build a community around your Airbnb. Sharing stories or special moments, like a guest who just got engaged at your property or a spectacular sunset view from your garden, gives a personal touch that potential customers may find appealing to guests.

Another effective strategy is creating a blog or a website for your property. This can be a platform where you delve deeper into what makes your space special, share more about the local area, and offer travel tips and insights. A blog improves your search engine visibility and positions you as a knowledgeable host passionate about providing great experiences.

Another method you might utilize to strengthen your online presence is email marketing. Collecting email addresses from past guests (with their permission) and sending out regular newsletters about your property, special offers, or local events keeps your rental top of mind. This direct channel of contact can be especially effective for encouraging repeat bookings.

Networking is also part of building a strong online presence. Connect with other Airbnb hosts, local tourism boards, or travel influencers. Engaging with their content, participating in online forums, and even collaborating on promotions can expand your reach and bring new eyes to your listing.

User-generated content can be a gold mine. Please encourage your guests to share their experiences online and tag your property. Whether a photo of their morning coffee on the balcony or a tweet about a great local restaurant you recommended, this content can greatly enhance your online credibility and appeal.

Online reviews play a critical role. Please encourage your guests to leave reviews and respond to each one, whether positive or negative. This shows that you value feedback and that you're an active and responsive host. Positive evaluations can greatly increase your internet visibility and attract new guests.

Lastly, keep up with online trends and adapt your strategy accordingly. Whether trying out new social media platforms or various content formats, maintaining a current profile will help you stay active and engaging.

Building a strong online presence as an Airbnb host involves a combination of a well-maintained Airbnb listing, active social media engagement, content creation, direct communication, networking, and leveraging guest content. It's about creating an online identity that truly reflects the experience you offer and connects with guests on multiple levels. Having a strong internet presence allows you to draw consumers more guests, build lasting relationships, and establish a successful and sustainable Airbnb business.

Chapter 7

MANAGING YOUR AIRBNB BUSINESS

Time management and scheduling are essential for an Airbnb host, akin to juggling multiple balls in the air. With guests coming and going, cleaning to arrange, and inquiries to respond to, managing your time effectively can make the difference between a smoothly running operation and a chaotic one.

One of the first steps in mastering time management is setting an explicit schedule for your Airbnb activities. This involves more than just blocking out dates on your calendar when your space is available. It means planning for the time needed to clean and prepare your space before each guest arrives, responding to inquiries and messages promptly, and ensuring you have enough time for regular maintenance and updates to your property.

Effective scheduling also means being realistic about how much you can handle. If you're juggling Airbnb hosting with a full-time job or other commitments, it's essential to understand your limits. Overextending yourself can lead to burnout and may negatively impact the quality of your hosting. Limiting bookings to weekends or certain times of the year when you know you can dedicate time and attention to your guests.

Automating specific tasks can be a lifesaver. Using Airbnb's automated messaging system to send out standard messages for booking confirmations, check-in instructions, and check-out reminders can save you a lot of time. Investing in a smart lock system for self-check-ins and check-outs can also streamline the process, reducing the time you need to be physically present.

Delegation is another crucial aspect of effective time management. If cleaning and preparing your space between guests is too time-consuming, consider hiring a professional cleaning service. This not only frees up your time but also ensures a consistent level of cleanliness and preparation for your guests.

Prioritizing tasks is also crucial. Not all tasks are created equal, and understanding which ones require immediate attention and which ones can wait is essential. For instance, responding to a new booking inquiry is more urgent than updating your listing photos. Creating a to-do list and categorizing tasks based on their urgency and importance can help you stay focused and efficient.

Setting aside specific times of the day to handle Airbnb-related tasks can also help you stay organized and prevent Airbnb from taking over your life. For example, you can respond to messages first thing in the morning or review your listings every Sunday afternoon. Having a routine can make managing your tasks more manageable.

Additionally, it's essential to plan for the unexpected. Guests might have special requests, accidents, and last-minute bookings can occur. A flexible yet structured schedule allows you to handle these surprises without too much stress.

Lastly, remember to allocate time for yourself. Hosting can be demanding, and taking care of your well-being is crucial for sustaining your energy and enthusiasm as a host. Whether setting aside time for hobbies, spending time with family, or relaxing, ensure you dedicate only some of your time to hosting.

In summary, effective time management and scheduling as an Airbnb host involve planning, prioritizing, automating, delegating, and flexibility. It's about finding a balance that allows you to manage your hosting responsibilities efficiently while enjoying the experience and maintaining your personal life. With good time management, you can run a successful Airbnb business without it running you.

Handling bookings, check-ins, and check-outs

Handling bookings, check-ins, and check-outs is crucial to the Airbnb hosting experience. While seemingly straightforward, these interactions are pivotal moments in your guests' journey and can significantly influence their overall impression of their stay.

Starting with bookings, how you manage these can set the tone for the entire guest experience. Promptly responding to booking inquiries shows potential guests that you are attentive and considerate, increasing their likelihood of choosing your space. It's essential to be clear and detailed in your communication, answering any questions they might have and providing them with all the necessary information about your space. This helps in building trust and setting clear expectations from the outset.

Once a booking is confirmed, the next crucial step is the check-in process. This is the first real-life interaction your guests will have with your space, and making it as smooth and welcoming as possible is critical. If you're meeting guests in person, this is an excellent opportunity to make a warm first impression. A brief tour of the space, highlighting any unique features or instructions, can be beneficial. Ensuring the process is easy and secure for hosts who prefer or need to offer self-check-in is essential. Providing clear instructions, with photos or a short video, can guide guests through the process.

During their stay, being available to answer questions or address issues is part of good hosting. Quick and helpful responses can enhance your guests' experience and show you're considerate and attentive hosts.

Check-out is the final step in the guests' journey and is just as crucial as check-in. Communicating check-out procedures and times is essential for a smooth transition. For instance, instructions on where to leave keys, how to lock up, and what to do with used linens can be handy. Offering a flexible check-out time can also be a nice gesture that guests often appreciate.

After check-out, following up with a thank you message can add a personal touch to the experience. This leaves a positive, lasting impression and encourages guests to leave a review of their stay. Reviews are vital in the Airbnb community, and a simple reminder or thank you can prompt guests to leave their feedback.

Handling issues arising during these stages with professionalism and empathy is also crucial. Whether it's a last-minute booking alteration, a problem during check-in, or a guest who's accidentally taken the keys with them, being prepared to handle such situations calmly and effectively can make all the difference.

It's also beneficial to continuously seek ways to improve these processes based on guest feedback and your own experiences. Maybe guests often ask the same questions at check-in, suggesting you include more information in your welcome message. Or there's a way to streamline your check-out process to make it easier for you and your guests.

Handling bookings, check-ins, and check-outs is more than managing reservations. It's about creating a seamless and welcoming experience for your guests from when they book to when they leave. By focusing on clear communication, convenience, and personal touches, you can ensure that these crucial aspects of the guest's journey contribute positively to their overall experience and your success as an Airbnb host.

Outsourcing tasks if needed

Outsourcing tasks as an Airbnb host can be a game-changer, especially when hosting demands overlap with your personal life or other professional commitments. It's about recognizing that sometimes, enlisting help is beneficial and necessary to maintain the quality of your hosting and the balance in your life.

One of the most common tasks to outsource is cleaning. Ensuring your rental is spotlessly clean for each new guest is crucial but can also be time-consuming. Hiring a professional cleaning service can relieve you of this burden. These services are often familiar with the specific needs of Airbnb rentals, such as quick turnovers and attention to detail. Not only does this free up your time, but it also often results in a higher standard of cleanliness, which is a significant factor in guest satisfaction and positive reviews.

Another area where outsourcing can be helpful is property maintenance. Regular upkeep, like lawn care, pool maintenance, or fixing wear and tear, is essential for keeping your property attractive and functional. Hiring professionals to handle these tasks ensures they are done correctly and promptly, which is particularly important if you manage the property remotely or have multiple listings.

If your Airbnb activity is high, considering a property management service might be worth it. These services handle everything from bookings to guest communication, check-ins, and cleaning. While this comes with a cost, it can be a worthwhile investment, especially if it means your Airbnb can operate smoothly without requiring your constant attention.

Digital tasks, like updating your listing, managing your bookings, or even handling your Airbnb-related social media, can also be outsourced. Virtual assistants or freelancers with experience in hospitality and social media management can take on these roles, ensuring your online presence and guest communications are handled efficiently.

Outsourcing doesn't mean losing the personal touch that often sets Airbnb hosts apart. You can still be involved in your property's critical decisions and overall management. It's about delegating time-consuming or specialized tasks to others while focusing on aspects of hosting that you enjoy or are crucial for your business model.

Selecting the right people or services is crucial when you decide to outsource. Look for individuals or companies with good reviews and a track record in the hospitality industry. Clear communication of your expectations and standards is essential. Remember, these individuals or services are an extension of you as a host, so their work directly reflects on you and your Airbnb.

Also, consider the financial aspect. Outsourcing is an additional expense, so weighing the costs against the benefits is essential. Will hiring a cleaning service allow you to host more often, thus increasing your income? Will a property management service enhance guest satisfaction, leading to better reviews and more bookings? Analyzing these factors is crucial to ensure that outsourcing makes sense for your business.

Outsourcing tasks as an Airbnb host can be a strategic move to enhance the quality of your hosting, maintain high standards, and manage your time more effectively. Whether it's cleaning, maintenance, management, or digital tasks, delegating these responsibilities can help you run your Airbnb business more efficiently and with less personal strain. By choosing the right services and maintaining clear communication, you can ensure that outsourcing contributes positively to your Airbnb's success and your satisfaction as a host.

Chapter 8

SCALING YOUR AIRBNB BUSINESS

Expanding to multiple properties in the Airbnb business is like stepping into a larger world filled with new opportunities and challenges. It's transitioning from being a host with a single listing to managing a small business. This move can significantly increase your income potential and allow you to reach a broader range of guests, but it also requires careful planning, organization, and scaling of your operations.

When considering expansion, the first step is to assess your current hosting experience. Have you successfully managed one property? Are you comfortable with the demands of being an Airbnb host, and do you enjoy it? This self-assessment is crucial because working on multiple properties amplifies the responsibilities and tasks.

Finding the suitable properties is the next crucial step. This involves more than just liking a property; it requires market research to understand what properties are in demand in different areas. Are travelers looking for cozy downtown apartments, or are they searching for secluded country homes? Each property type has its market, and understanding these dynamics is critical to intelligent investments.

Financial planning cannot be overstated. Expanding to multiple properties involves a significant investment in purchasing or leasing properties and furnishing, maintenance, and possibly higher operational costs. A solid financial plan that includes budgets for these expenses and projections for potential income is essential. This plan should also account for periods of low occupancy and other unforeseen costs.

Once you have multiple properties, organization, and time management become even more crucial. Each property will have its bookings, maintenance needs, and guest communications. Property management software can streamline these processes, allowing you to manage multiple listings from one platform. This can include syncing booking calendars, automating messages, and keeping track of maintenance tasks.

Hiring a team might also become necessary. This could include cleaners, maintenance workers, or even a property manager if the scale of your operations justifies it. Building a reliable and efficient team is critical, as they will help ensure your properties are well-maintained and your guests are satisfied.

Marketing each property effectively is also essential. Each property should have its unique appeal and be dealt with accordingly. Tailoring your listings to highlight the distinctive features of each property, such as a fantastic view, a kid-friendly garden, or proximity to tourist attractions, can help attract the right guests.

Guest experience remains at the heart of Airbnb hosting, even when managing multiple properties. Ensuring each guest has a memorable stay is as important as ever. This might mean creating unique guidebooks for each property, being responsive to guests' needs, and maintaining high standards of cleanliness and comfort across all your properties.

Monitoring and adapting based on feedback and performance is critical to success. Keep track of how each property performs regarding occupancy rates, guest reviews, and income. Use this data to make informed pricing, marketing, and improvement decisions.

Expanding to multiple properties in the Airbnb market is an exciting step with increased income potential and new challenges. It requires careful planning, financial investment, efficient organization, effective marketing, and a focus on guest experience. Whether you're managing two properties or ten, the core principles of successful Airbnb hosting – providing great guest experiences, maintaining high standards, and efficient management – remain the same. Expanding your Airbnb business can be a rewarding and profitable venture with the right approach.

Hiring staff and managing a team

Hiring staff and managing a team are significant steps in scaling your Airbnb business. It marks a transition from being a solo host to becoming a manager or small business owner. This expansion can bring new levels of success to your Airbnb venture, but it also introduces the complexities of human resources management.

The decision to hire staff usually comes when the demands of managing your Airbnb - or multiple Airbnb - exceed what you can handle alone. It could start with hiring a cleaner to prepare your property between guests, or you might need someone to take guest communication, especially if you have listings in different time zones. As your business grows, roles might expand to include maintenance personnel, property managers, or marketing specialists.

The process of hiring starts with identifying the roles you need to fill. Each role should have a clear job description outlining the responsibilities, required skills, and expected outcomes. For example, a cleaner's role would involve cleaning, restocking supplies, and reporting any damage or maintenance needs.

Finding the right people is crucial. Look for candidates who have the necessary skills and fit the ethos and culture of your Airbnb business. Remember, these individuals will represent you and your brand to your guests. Depending on the role, you might want staff with hospitality experience or someone with a service-oriented attitude and good communication skills.

Once you have a team, managing them effectively is critical to ensuring your Airbnb runs smoothly. This involves more than just scheduling shifts and assigning tasks. It's about creating a collaborative and positive work environment. Regular communication is vital, whether it's through team meetings, email updates, or a group chat. Keeping everyone informed and aligned on expectations, guest experiences, and operational changes is essential.

Training your team is also a critical aspect of management. Each team member should be well-versed in their role, understand the standards of your Airbnb, and be equipped to handle situations that may arise. This might involve training sessions, written guidelines, or shadowing you or another experienced team member.

Feedback and evaluation are essential parts of team management. Regularly reviewing your team's performance, providing constructive feedback, and recognizing their efforts can significantly enhance their productivity and job satisfaction. Encourage your team to provide feedback as well - they might have insights into operations or guest experiences that you still need to consider.

Delegating effectively is another skill to hone. As a host-turned-manager, letting go of specific tasks can be challenging, but it's necessary for the growth of your business. Trust your team to handle their responsibilities, but be available for support and guidance when needed.

Handling conflicts or issues within the team is also part of management. Addressing problems promptly and fairly and finding solutions helps maintain a positive working environment.

Lastly, remember that your role as a manager is to oversee operations and lead and inspire your team. Your enthusiasm for providing excellent guest experiences should be infectious. A motivated team aligned with your vision and goals can significantly contribute to the success and growth of your Airbnb business.

Hiring staff and managing a team is crucial to growing your Airbnb business. It involves identifying your needed roles, hiring the right people, training them, driving them effectively, and providing leadership. With a strong team, you can ensure that your Airbnb or multiple Airbnb's operate smoothly, guest satisfaction remains high, and your business thrives.

Maximizing profitability

Maximizing profitability in the Airbnb business is like navigating a ship through changing seas. It requires skill, adaptability, and a keen understanding of your vessel and the waters you're sailing in. For Airbnb hosts, this means attracting guests and optimizing every aspect of your business to ensure you're getting the most out of your investment.

The first step in maximizing profitability is understanding your market. Just like a shopkeeper who knows what products are in demand, as an Airbnb host, you must understand what guests in your area are looking for. This could mean tailoring your space to appeal to business travelers in a city center or making your property family-friendly if you're in a vacation destination. Keeping an eye on travel trends and guest preferences can inform how you set up and market your space.

Pricing strategy plays a crucial role in profitability. Setting the right price for your rental is a delicate balance – too high, and you might deter potential guests; too low, and you're leaving money on the table. Utilize dynamic pricing tools that adjust your rates based on demand, seasonality, and local events. These tools can help ensure you maximize your income potential on any night.

Another critical aspect is maximizing occupancy. An empty rental doesn't generate income, so minimizing those gaps is essential. This might mean adjusting your minimum stay requirements or offering last-minute discounts to fill in open dates. Also, consider diversifying your marketing and using multiple platforms to reach a wider audience.

Improving guest experience can also lead to higher profitability. Happy guests are more likely to leave positive reviews, recommend your place to others, and return for another stay. Small touches like a welcome basket, a local guidebook you've created, or personalized recommendations can make a big difference. These efforts can elevate your listing, allowing you to justify a higher price and attract repeat business.

Operational efficiency is another area to focus on. Reducing costs where possible without compromising on quality is critical. This could involve energy-saving measures, cost-effective yet high-quality furnishings, or finding the best deals for amenities like internet or cable TV. Streamlining cleaning and maintenance processes, possibly through trusted contractors, can save time and money.

Additionally, understanding and minimizing your tax liabilities is part of maximizing profitability. Keep track of all your expenses related to your Airbnb – from cleaning supplies to repairs – as these can often be deducted from your income come tax time. Consulting with a tax professional who understands the nuances of rental income can be a worthwhile investment.

Leveraging your Airbnb income to further invest in your property or acquire additional properties is another way to increase profitability. This could mean upgrading your current space to attract a higher-paying market segment or expanding your portfolio to include more properties.

Lastly, staying adaptable and willing to evolve your business strategy is crucial in the ever-changing landscape of short-term rentals. Keeping an eye on industry trends, guest feedback, and your performance data will help you make informed decisions and stay ahead of the curve.

Maximizing profitability as an Airbnb host involves a combination of strategic pricing, occupancy optimization, guest experience enhancement, operational efficiency, tax-savvy, and continuous adaptation and investment. By focusing on these areas, you can turn your Airbnb venture from just a source of income into a profitable, sustainable business.

Chapter 9

SUCCESS STORIES AND CASE STUDIES

Delving into the stories of successful Airbnb hosts offers a window into the diverse and dynamic world of short-term rentals. These real-life examples are not just stories of financial success; they are tales of creativity, perseverance, and the ability to create memorable experiences for guests from around the globe.

One such story is that of Sarah and John, a couple who transformed an old, rundown farmhouse in rural France into a sought-after Airbnb destination. It was in disrepair when they first purchased the property, but they saw potential in its rustic charm and scenic location. They spent months renovating it, preserving its historic character while adding modern comforts. They marketed their Airbnb as a peaceful retreat in the countryside, complete with home-cooked meals using ingredients from their garden. Their attention to detail and the unique experience they offered quickly garnered rave reviews, leading to a steady stream of guests seeking a tranquil getaway.

Then there's the story of Carlos, who turned his small downtown Lisbon apartment into a tourist hotspot. Carlos, a graphic designer by trade, used his skills to create a visually stunning space with a quirky, artistic vibe. He also leveraged his knowledge of the city to curate a guidebook for his guests, highlighting off-the-beaten-path eateries and cultural events. His apartment was consistently booked out months in advance, thanks to his eye for design and ability to offer an insider's view of Lisbon.

In New York City, Mia's story stands out. She started with a tiny studio apartment in Brooklyn, which she listed on Airbnb to help pay her rent. Realizing the demand for affordable yet stylish accommodations in the city, Mia gradually expanded her Airbnb business, renting and managing several apartments in the area. She had a knack for creating cozy, Instagram-worthy spaces that appealed to young travelers seeking an authentic New York experience. Her business insight and understanding of her target market turned her Airbnb side hustle into a full-time, profitable venture.

Another inspiring example is Akira in Tokyo. A former hotelier, Akira brought his hospitality experience to his Airbnb listings. He offered a range of properties, from compact city apartments to traditional Japanese homes. What set Akira apart was his commitment to service. He provided his guests with a personal welcome, comprehensive local guides, and even organized tours around the city. His dedication to offering an exceptional guest experience earned him a reputation as one of the top hosts in Tokyo.

In Bali, the story of Kadek highlights the impact of Airbnb on local communities. Kadek started with a small guesthouse built on his family's land. With a deep understanding of Balinese culture and a passion for sharing it, Kadek created an experience beyond just a place to stay. He guests to participate in local ceremonies, learn about traditional farming practices, and enjoy homemade Balinese meals. His Airbnb became a popular choice for travelers seeking cultural immersion and provided a source of income for his community.

These stories illustrate the diverse paths to success in Airbnb hosting. From renovating historic properties and leveraging personal skills to delivering exceptional customer service and embracing local culture, these hosts have created thriving businesses. Their experiences show that success in Airbnb hosting comes not just from the property itself but from the host's expertise, creativity, and dedication. Each of these hosts has found a way to stand out in the crowded Airbnb market, offering unique stays that resonate with their guests, ultimately leading to successful and rewarding hosting experiences.

Lessons learned and insights from experienced hosts

Gathering lessons and insights from experienced Airbnb hosts is like tapping into a rich mine of wisdom. Through their journey of trials, successes, and continuous learning, these hosts offer invaluable advice for anyone embarking on or navigating the world of Airbnb hosting.

One of the fundamental lessons seasoned hosts share is the importance of setting clear expectations. This starts right from your listing - ensuring that every description and image accurately represents your space. Experienced hosts emphasize honesty; it's better to undersell and overdeliver than to disappoint your guests. This approach builds trust and often leads to better reviews, as guests appreciate transparency.

Another critical insight is the significance of responsiveness and communication. Time and again, successful hosts talk about the positive impact of responding quickly to inquiries and proactively communicating with guests before and during their stay. This enhances the guest experience and boosts your visibility on platforms like Airbnb, where response rates matter.

Personalization is another recurring theme. Adding personal touches, such as a welcome note, a small gift, or custom recommendations for local experiences, can make a big difference. These small gestures show guests that you care about their experience and are willing to go the extra mile to ensure they have a memorable stay.

Experienced hosts also often discuss the importance of seeking and acting on feedback. Encouraging guests to provide honest reviews and taking their suggestions seriously is crucial. Whether it's a recommendation for a new coffee maker or a tip on improving the check-in process, this feedback can be a goldmine of information for enhancing your hosting game.

Flexibility is another lesson that many hosts learn over time. Being flexible with check-in and check-out times, accommodating last-minute requests, or adjusting your cancellation policy can significantly enhance your appeal to potential guests. Of course, balancing this with your own convenience and policies is crucial.

Regular updating and maintenance of the property is something that experienced hosts consistently prioritize. Keeping the space in top condition ensures good reviews and prevents more significant maintenance issues down the line. This could mean regular deep cleaning, updating décor, or fixing minor problems before they become substantial.

A fascinating insight from long-term hosts is the importance of creating a manual or guide for guests. A comprehensive guide with appliance instructions, tips for navigating the local area, emergency contact information, and house rules can significantly improve the guest experience. It reduces confusion and the need for guests to contact you for small queries.

Many seasoned hosts also discuss the importance of understanding and complying with local regulations. Staying informed about the legal aspects of Airbnb hosting, including taxes, permits, and insurance, is crucial for compliance and peace of mind.

Finally, experienced hosts often emphasize the need for self-care and setting boundaries. Hosting can be demanding, and getting caught up in trying to provide the perfect experience is easy. Successful hosts learn to find a balance, setting boundaries that allow them to enjoy hosting without it taking over their lives.

The lessons and insights from experienced Airbnb hosts are diverse, but they all point toward creating a sustainable, enjoyable, and successful hosting experience. From honesty in listings, responsiveness, and personalization to seeking feedback, regular maintenance, and legal compliance, these insights are invaluable for new and seasoned hosts. Balancing guests' needs with your own, continuously improving your offering, and managing the business aspects efficiently is critical to thriving in the world of Airbnb hosting.

Chapter 10

TROUBLESHOOTING AND PROBLEM SOLVING

Delving into Airbnb hosting is an adventure filled with unexpected twists and turns. While it offers a world of opportunities, it also comes with its fair share of challenges and common issues that hosts must navigate.

One of the most common challenges is managing guest expectations. Guests come with diverse needs and wants; sometimes, what they expect might not align with what you offer. This discrepancy can lead to dissatisfaction, no matter how impeccable your service is. Clear and honest communication about what guests can expect in your listing is crucial. Providing detailed descriptions, accurate photos, and prompt responses to queries can help align guests' expectations with reality.

Another frequent issue is the upkeep and maintenance of the property. Wear and tear are inevitable; you might encounter everything from minor breakages to significant maintenance needs. Staying on top of these issues is essential, not just for guest satisfaction but also for the longevity of your property. Regular inspections and having a network of reliable tradespeople for quick fixes can be invaluable.

Dealing with demanding guests is another challenge that hosts sometimes face. You may encounter guests who are noisy, disrespectful to your property, or unjustly leave negative reviews. Handling such situations requires a mix of diplomacy, firmness, and, sometimes, intervention from Airbnb's support team. Having clear house rules and proactively communicating with guests during their stay can help mitigate these issues.

Then, there's the challenge of achieving and maintaining high ratings. Guest reviews significantly impact your visibility and attractiveness on Airbnb. Negative reviews, particularly those that are unfair or misleading, can be frustrating. Responding professionally to all reviews, addressing criticisms, and continually improving your service based on feedback is essential for maintaining a good rating.

Seasonal fluctuations in demand can also pose a challenge. There might be times of the year when bookings are scarce, which can affect your income. Diversifying your marketing efforts, adjusting your pricing strategy during off-peak seasons, and targeting different types of guests can help maintain a steady flow of bookings.

Cancellation and no-shows are other issues hosts often deal with. While Airbnb has policies in place, dealing with last-minute cancellations or guests who don't turn up can be inconvenient and financially impactful. A transparent and fair cancellation policy and overbooking strategies can help manage these situations.

Understanding and complying with local laws and regulations is another hurdle. This includes zoning laws, licensing requirements, and tax obligations. Navigating these legalities can be complex and time-consuming, but it is essential for legal and hassle-free hosting.

In some cases, hosts also face challenges with their neighbors or community. Only some people are enthusiastic about having short-term rentals in their neighborhood. Complaints from neighbors about noise, parking, or the constant flow of strangers can be challenging to handle. Being respectful and communicative with your neighbors and ensuring your guests know and adhere to community norms can help mitigate such issues.

Finally, balancing personal time and Airbnb hosting responsibilities can be demanding, especially for those who manage their properties alongside other commitments. It's easy to underestimate the time and effort required to execute an Airbnb property effectively. Learning to delegate tasks, using automation tools, and setting boundaries for your availability are critical to maintaining this balance.

Airbnb hosting, while rewarding, comes with its set of everyday challenges, from managing guest expectations and property maintenance to dealing with demanding guests and navigating legal requirements. Successful hosts learn to navigate these challenges with patience, strategic planning, clear communication, and a continuous focus on improving their service. It's a journey that requires adaptability, resilience, and a commitment to creating positive guest experiences.

Solutions and best practices

Navigating the world of Airbnb hosting involves encountering various challenges, but with every challenge comes a solution and a set of best practices that can guide hosts toward a more prosperous and less stressful experience.

When it comes to managing guest expectations, clarity is critical. Ensuring your listing accurately reflects what your space offers is crucial. This means detailed descriptions, honest portrayal of the space through photos, and quick, clear communication with potential guests. When guests know exactly what to expect, there's less room for disappointment.

Upkeep and maintenance are ongoing tasks in the life of an Airbnb host. Regular inspections and maintenance of the property keep it in top condition and prevent more significant issues down the line. Creating a maintenance schedule and sticking to it can be helpful. Also, building a good relationship with reliable local tradespeople means you have someone to call when unexpected repairs are needed.

Dealing with demanding guests is a less pleasant aspect of hosting, but many hosts need help with it. The best approach is to remain professional and calm. Clear house rules from the start can be a reference point if issues arise. If a situation escalates, don't hesitate to involve Airbnb's support team, who are there to help resolve conflicts.

Maintaining high ratings is crucial in the competitive world of Airbnb. Encouraging guests to leave reviews and responding to all positive and negative reviews is essential. If you receive a negative review, respond professionally and take any feedback as an opportunity to improve. Enhancing your space and service based on guest feedback can improve reviews.

Flexibility in pricing and targeting different guest segments can be adequate to manage seasonal fluctuations. Lowering prices during off-peak times or offering special deals can attract guests. Also, tailoring your space or marketing to appeal to different types of guests, such as business travelers or families, depending on the season, can help maintain a steady flow of bookings.

Cancellation and no-shows are frustrating, but a clear cancellation policy can mitigate these issues. Choose a policy that strikes a balance between flexibility for guests and protection for you as a host. Like those used by hotels, overbooking strategies can also be a backup plan, but they must be managed carefully to avoid double-booking.

Legal compliance is non-negotiable. Staying informed about local laws and regulations related to short-term rentals and seeking advice from professionals in areas like tax and real estate law can ensure you're running your Airbnb legally and smoothly.

Maintaining a good relationship with your neighbors is also important. Keeping them informed about your Airbnb, considering their concerns, and ensuring your guests respect the neighborhood can help prevent conflicts. Clear guidelines for guests about noise levels and parking can alleviate common neighbor concerns.

Finally, balancing personal time with hosting responsibilities is crucial for long-term success and emotional well-being. Automation tools for messaging, scheduling, and pricing can save time. Delegating tasks like cleaning and maintenance can also help. Setting aside time for yourself and your family is essential, ensuring that hosting doesn't take over your life.

While Airbnb hosting comes with its challenges, there are solutions and best practices that can help navigate these issues. From clear communication and regular maintenance to professional handling of difficult situations and legal compliance, these practices ensure a high-quality experience for your guests while making the hosting process as smooth and enjoyable as possible. With the right approach, Airbnb hosting can be a rewarding and sustainable venture.

Chapter 11

FUTURE TRENDS IN AIRBNB HOSTING

The short-term rental industry constantly evolves, with emerging trends and innovations shaping how hosts interact with guests and manage their properties. Staying abreast of these changes is crucial for hosts looking to remain competitive and offer the best possible experience to their guests.

One significant trend is the increasing demand for unique and experiential stays. Guests seek more than just a place to sleep; they seek accommodations that offer a unique experience or connect them with local culture. This could be anything from a treehouse or a converted barn to a city apartment filled with local art. Hosts who can offer these unique experiences are likely to attract more bookings.

Technology plays a more significant role than ever in the short-term rental industry. Smart home technology, for instance, is becoming increasingly popular. Features like keyless entry, smart thermostats, and voice-controlled devices enhance guest convenience and help hosts manage their properties efficiently. These technologies can improve energy efficiency, provide better security, and offer guests a more seamless stay.

Another emerging trend is the focus on sustainable and eco-friendly practices. More guests are looking for environmentally responsible lodging options. This includes properties with features like solar panels, recycling facilities, and eco-friendly toiletries. Hosts who embrace these practices contribute to environmental conservation and appeal to a growing segment of eco-conscious travelers.

The personalization of guest experiences is also gaining traction. With the help of data analytics and AI, hosts can now offer more personalized services to guests. From tailored recommendations for local dining and experiences to personalized welcome messages, this level of personalization can significantly enhance the guest experience.

In response to the global health crisis, there has also been a shift towards more flexible booking and cancellation policies. Guests now value the ability to change or cancel their bookings without hefty penalties. Hosts offering these flexible policies will likely be more attractive to cautious travelers.

The rise of remote work has also impacted the short-term rental market. With more people working remotely, there's an increasing demand for rentals that cater to this lifestyle. This means properties with dedicated workspaces, reliable high-speed internet, and amenities for more extended stays are in higher demand.

Additionally, the industry's use of virtual and augmented reality is on the rise. These technologies can offer potential guests a more immersive view of the property before they book, which can be particularly useful for those booking from afar.

Hosts are also finding innovative ways to manage and market their properties. Technology is at the forefront of these innovations, from using social media platforms to showcase their spaces to utilizing property management software for efficient operations.

Community building is another trend gaining momentum. Hosts are creating communities around their properties, offering experiences connecting guests with each other and the local area.

This could be through organized events, community dinners, or guided tours.

The short-term rental industry is evolving rapidly, driven by technological advancements, changing guest preferences, and broader global trends. Hosts who keep up with these trends and adapt accordingly can enhance their guests' experiences, improve their operations, and drive more bookings. Whether it's through offering unique stays, embracing technology, focusing on sustainability, or personalizing the guest experience, staying ahead of these trends is critical to succeeding in the dynamic world of Airbnb hosting.

Preparing for the future

Preparing for the future in Airbnb hosting is akin to setting sail for uncharted waters. It requires foresight, adaptability, and a willingness to embrace new trends and technologies. Short-term rentals are ever-evolving, and staying ahead of the curve is crucial for continued success.

One of the critical aspects of preparing for the future is embracing technology. The rise of smart home devices, from digital thermostats to keyless entry systems, is changing how hosts manage their properties. These technologies enhance the guest experience by offering convenience and efficiency and help hosts monitor and maintain their properties remotely. Keeping abreast of technological advancements and incorporating them into your property can set you apart.

Another important consideration is the growing emphasis on sustainability. With increasing number of travelers becoming environmentally conscious, incorporating eco-friendly practices into your hosting can be a significant draw. This could involve anything from installing energy-efficient appliances and using renewable energy sources to providing recycling facilities and eco-friendly cleaning products. Adopting these practices appeals to a growing segment of eco-conscious guests and contributes to a more sustainable future.

Staying informed about changes in the travel and tourism industry is also vital. The preferences and behaviors of travelers are constantly shifting, influenced by factors like demographics, economic trends, and global events. Keeping a finger on the pulse of these changes can help you anticipate future demands and adjust your offerings accordingly.

The ongoing impact of global health events has underscored the importance of flexibility and adaptability in the short-term rental market. This includes offering flexible cancellation policies, adapting your space to cater to longer-term stays, or pivoting to target different types of travelers, such as remote workers or staycations. Adapting to changing circumstances quickly is critical to maintaining a successful Airbnb business in uncertain times.

Personalization will continue to play a significant role in the future of Airbnb hosting. As technology advances, so does the ability to gather and analyze data about guests' preferences and behaviors. This can allow for more personalized communication and offerings, enhancing the guest experience and setting your property apart.

Networking and community involvement are also important. Building relationships with other hosts, local businesses, and community members can provide valuable support and insights. This network can be a source of referrals, advice, and collaboration, which can be particularly beneficial as the market evolves.

Additionally, continuous learning and development should be a part of your strategy for the future. This could involve taking courses on hospitality management, staying updated on the latest marketing strategies, or learning about new property maintenance techniques. Investing in your education and skills ensures you're well-equipped to handle the challenges and opportunities that the future holds.

Finally, remember the importance of financial planning. The short-term rental market can be unpredictable, and a solid financial plan can help you navigate periods of fluctuation. This might involve setting aside some of your earnings for future investments, maintenance, or as a buffer during leaner times.

preparing for the future in Airbnb hosting involves embracing technology, adopting sustainable practices, staying informed about industry trends, being adaptable, personalizing the guest experience, building a solid network, continuously learning, and sound financial planning. By focusing on these areas, you can ensure that your Airbnb business not only survives but thrives in the years to come, adapting to whatever the future may bring.

CONCLUSION

Recapping the critical points in the context of Airbnb hosting provides a comprehensive overview of what it takes to be successful in this dynamic field. Here's a summary of the essential elements:

1. **Managing Guest Expectations**: Ensuring your listing accurately reflects your space is crucial. Clear, honest descriptions and photos help align guest expectations with reality, leading to greater satisfaction.

2. **Property Upkeep and Maintenance**: Regular maintenance and addressing issues promptly are essential. This keeps your property in top condition and enhances guest experiences.

3. **Dealing with Difficult Guests**: Adopt a professional and calm approach. Clear house rules and Airbnb's support team can help resolve conflicts.

4. **Maintaining High Ratings**: Encourage guest reviews and respond to all feedback professionally. Continuous improvement based on this feedback is critical.

5. **Managing Seasonal Fluctuations**: Adjusting pricing and targeting different guest segments during off-peak seasons can help maintain steady bookings.

6. **Cancellation and No-Shows**: A transparent and fair cancellation policy can mitigate these issues. Overbooking strategies can be a backup but require careful management.

7. **Legal Compliance**: Stay informed about and comply with local laws and regulations related to short-term rentals, including taxes and permits.

8. **Neighborhood Relations**: Being considerate and communicative with neighbors helps prevent conflicts. Ensure guests respect neighborhood norms.

9. **Balancing Personal Time**: Use automation tools and delegate tasks to balance personal life and hosting responsibilities.

10. **Embracing Technology**: Incorporate smart home devices and stay abreast of technological advancements to enhance guest experiences and operational efficiency.

11. **Sustainability Practices**: Adopting eco-friendly measures appeals to a growing segment of environmentally conscious travelers and contributes to sustainability.

12. **Adapting to Industry Changes**: Keep up with travel trends and guest behavior to adjust your offerings and stay competitive.

13. **Personalization**: Use data and technology to offer personalized experiences, enhancing guest satisfaction.

14. **Networking and Community Involvement**: Build relationships with other hosts, local businesses, and community members for support and collaboration.

15. **Continuous Learning and Development**: Keep learning about hospitality management, marketing, and maintenance to improve your skills and knowledge.

16. **Financial Planning**: Ensure sound financial management to navigate fluctuating market conditions and plan for future investments.

Successful Airbnb hosting requires a blend of good communication, property management, adaptability, technological savvy, and personal growth. Staying informed, being proactive, and continually striving to enhance the guest experience are the cornerstones of a thriving Airbnb business.

Encouragement and motivation for aspiring Airbnb hosts

Embarking on becoming an Airbnb host can feel like stepping into a new world filled with opportunities and challenges. If you're considering this path or have just started, embracing the adventure ahead with optimism and determination is essential.

First and foremost, remember that every successful Airbnb host started right where you are now. It's normal to feel excitement and apprehension, but know that you'll gain valuable experience with each step. Hosting on Airbnb is not just about earning extra income; it's an opportunity to meet people from diverse backgrounds, share your space and local knowledge, and contribute to making travel a more personal and memorable experience for others.

Think of your Airbnb as a canvas to express your creativity and hospitality. Whether it's through thoughtful decor, a warm welcome, or little extras like a local guidebook, you can create a unique and memorable experience for your guests. These personal touches often make the most significant impact and can turn guests into advocates for your space.

Embrace the learning curve that comes with being a new host. Every challenge is an opportunity to grow and improve. Whether it's mastering the art of creating a compelling listing, navigating guest communications, or handling the logistics of property management, each experience will make you a more skilled and confident host.

Remember, most rave reviews often come from hosts who go the extra mile. Being attentive to your guests' needs, maintaining high standards of cleanliness, and being responsive and helpful can set you apart. Even small gestures, like leaving a welcome note or providing extra amenities, can leave a lasting positive impression.

Networking with other hosts can be incredibly beneficial. Join local host groups or online communities where you can share experiences, get advice, and find support. These networks can be invaluable, especially when you're just starting. Learning from those who have been in your shoes can provide you with insights and inspiration.

Stay adaptable and open to feedback. The world of short-term rentals is dynamic, and being flexible can help you navigate its ebbs and flows. Listening to your guests' feedback and being willing to make changes based on their suggestions shows you are committed to providing the best possible experience.

Remember to underestimate the power of a positive attitude. Hosting can have stressful moments, but approaching challenges with a problem-solving mindset can make a difference. Your attitude can also influence your guests' experience, so a positive outlook can help ensure they leave with fond memories.

Finally, remember why you started. Whether it's to meet new people, earn extra income, or share the beauty of your location, keeping your initial motivations in mind can be a powerful source of inspiration and motivation.

Becoming an Airbnb host is a journey of learning, growth, and opportunities to connect with others. Embrace this adventure with enthusiasm and an open mind. With dedication, creativity, and a focus on providing great experiences, you can become not just a host but someone who adds a special touch to your guests' travels. So take a deep breath, step forward, and get ready to open your door to a world of possibilities.

How readers can get in touch with you for further assistance or resources

For readers looking to delve deeper into the world of Airbnb hosting, seeking further assistance, or desiring more resources, there are several ways you can reach out and connect for more information and support.

The first and most direct way to get in touch is through email. Emailing you can be a great starting point if you have specific questions, need advice, or are looking for personalized tips on becoming a successful Airbnb host. In your email, be clear about what you're looking for. Whether it's advice on improving your listing, dealing with a challenging guest situation, or understanding the nuances of Airbnb's policies, providing details will help give you targeted and helpful advice.

Another effective way to connect is through social media platforms. Many experienced Airbnb hosts have active profiles on Instagram, Facebook, or LinkedIn platforms. These platforms provide a way to get in touch and offer a wealth of information through posts, stories, and articles. You can follow these hosts, engage with their content, and reach out via direct messages for more personalized interactions.

Blogs and websites dedicated to Airbnb hosting are also valuable resources. These sites often have contact forms to submit your queries or request more detailed guides and resources. Additionally, many of these websites offer newsletters that you can subscribe to. These newsletters can be a goldmine of information, providing tips, industry updates, and insights to your inbox.

Participating in online forums and communities is another excellent way to connect. Platforms like Reddit, Quora, or specialized Airbnb hosting forums are places where hosts share their experiences and advice worldwide. You can post your questions, join discussions, and even connect with other hosts who can offer guidance based on their experiences.

If you want more structured support, consider attending webinars or online workshops. Many experienced hosts and industry experts conduct these sessions, and they can be incredibly insightful. These events provide valuable information and allow you to ask questions and interact with experts and fellow hosts.

For those who prefer more traditional methods, there's always the option of reaching out via phone or arranging in-person meetings, where feasible. A direct conversation can sometimes be more effective, especially for complex queries or in-depth discussions.

When reaching out for assistance or resources, respecting the hosts' time and expertise is essential. These individuals often share their knowledge and experience out of a passion for hosting and a desire to help others succeed.

You can contact experienced hosts or industry experts for further assistance or resources in your Airbnb hosting journey. Whether through email, social media, blogs, online forums, webinars, or direct calls and meetings, the Airbnb community is generally supportive and open to sharing insights. Don't hesitate to reach out, ask questions, and seek the help you need. Engaging with this community can significantly enhance your knowledge, provide practical solutions, and help you navigate the exciting world of Airbnb hosting with greater confidence and success.

APPENDIX

For Airbnb hosts, having access to a range of resources, templates, and checklists can be incredibly helpful in streamlining operations, ensuring consistency, and providing excellent guest experiences. Here's an overview of such tools and where you can find them:

1. **Templates for Guest Communication**: These include welcome messages, check-in instructions, house rules, local recommendations, and check-out instructions. You can create these based on your experiences or find examples online on hosting blogs or forums. Tailor them to your property and personal hosting style.

2. **Cleaning Checklists**: A comprehensive cleaning checklist ensures your property is spotless and ready for each new guest. This list should cover all areas of your property, including bedrooms, bathrooms, kitchen, living areas, and outdoor spaces. Websites dedicated to hosting and cleaning services often provide such checklists.

3. **Maintenance Checklists**: Regular maintenance is vital to maintaining your property. A checklist for routine maintenance tasks (like checking smoke detectors, servicing significant appliances, and seasonal tasks) can be invaluable. You can develop this over time based on the specific needs of your property.

4. **Inventory List**: Keeping track of all items in your Airbnb ensures that everything is present and is protected with your knowledge. This can be a simple spreadsheet that lists all items in each room.

5. **Welcome Book Template**: This can include information about your property, emergency contact numbers, appliance instructions, Wi-Fi details, and local recommendations.

Templates for welcome books are available online, or you can create a personalized one.

6. **Financial Management Templates**: For tracking your income, expenses, and taxes, financial templates can be handy. You can use essential accounting software or find spreadsheet templates specifically designed for rental properties online.

7. **Guest Review Templates**: While each review should be personalized, having a template can help streamline the process. You can find suggestions for structuring guest reviews on various hosting advice websites.

8. **Legal and Regulatory Checklists**: Depending on your location, specific legal and regulatory requirements for short-term rentals might exist. Creating a checklist of these requirements can help ensure you stay compliant.

9. **Booking and Reservation System**: While Airbnb's platform handles most of this, having your system for tracking bookings, especially if you list on multiple platforms, can be helpful. Look for online tools or software that can sync with different booking platforms.

10. **Emergency Procedures Guide**: A guide for dealing with emergencies, like power outages, medical emergencies, or natural disasters, is essential. This should be tailored to your property and location.

To find these resources, you can start by exploring:

· Airbnb's own resource center offers a range of guides and tips.

· Online forums and communities for Airbnb hosts.

· Websites and blogs dedicated to Airbnb hosting or property management.

· Professional organizations or local groups for vacation rental owners.

· YouTube channels that focus on Airbnb hosting tips and strategies.

While templates and checklists can provide a solid foundation, they should be adapted to suit your specific property and hosting style. Personalization is critical to creating a memorable and smooth experience for your guests.

Additional reading and references

For Airbnb hosts looking to deepen their understanding and enhance their skills, a wealth of additional reading and references is available. These resources can provide valuable insights, practical tips, and innovative strategies to elevate your hosting experience. Here are several types of resources that are worth exploring:

1. **Books on Hospitality and Customer Service**: Books like "The Heart of Hospitality: Great Hotel and Restaurant Leaders Share Their Secrets" by Micah Solomon or "Setting the Table: The Transforming Power of Hospitality in Business" by Danny Meyer offer insights into exceptional customer service and hospitality, which are critical components of successful Airbnb hosting.

2. **Real Estate Investment Books**: To understand the business aspect of Airbnb hosting, books like "The Book on Rental Property Investing" by Brandon Turner can be invaluable. They guide real estate investment, closely related to running a successful Airbnb.

3. **Airbnb Hosting Guides**: Look for books specifically about Airbnb hosting, such as "The Airbnb Story" by Leigh Gallagher, which offers both the history of the company and insights into successful hosting.

4. **Online Articles and Blogs**: Websites like AirDNA and the Airbnb Community Center offer many articles on best practices, market trends, and hosting tips. Blogs run by experienced hosts can also be a goldmine of practical advice and real-life experiences.

5. **Podcasts**: Several podcasts are dedicated to short-term rentals and Airbnb hosting. Listening to episodes from podcasts like "Get Paid for Your Pad" or "Thanks for Visiting" can provide you with tips, trends, and stories from other hosts.

6. **YouTube Channels**: Channels dedicated to Airbnb hosting or real estate can be informative and inspiring. They often feature tutorials, property tours, and interviews with successful hosts.

7. **Online Courses**: Platforms like Udemy or Skillshare offer courses on Airbnb hosting, real estate investment, and hospitality management. These courses range from beginner to advanced levels.

8. **Industry Reports and Market Analysis**: Understanding the market trends is crucial. Reports from sources like Statista or market analysis from AirDNA provide valuable data on travel trends, occupancy rates, and pricing strategies.

9. **Local Regulations and Legal Guides**: Stay informed about the legal aspects of Airbnb hosting in your area. This might involve reading local government publications or guides from legal experts in real estate.

10. **Forums and Community Groups**: Joining online forums or community groups where hosts share their experiences can be beneficial. Platforms like the Airbnb Community Forum or Reddit have active communities discussing various aspects of hosting.

11. **Travel and Tourism Literature**: To enhance the guest experience, reading up on travel trends and tourism

literature can be helpful. This helps in understanding what travelers are looking for in their stays.

12. **Interior Design and Home Improvement Resources**: For tips on property presentation and interior design, websites like Houzz or Pinterest, as well as home improvement blogs and magazines, can offer inspiration and practical ideas.

A wide array of resources are available for Airbnb hosts looking to expand their knowledge and improve their hosting skills. From books and online courses to podcasts and community forums, these resources cover various aspects of Airbnb hosting, including hospitality, real estate investment, market trends, and legal considerations. Engaging with these materials can provide valuable insights and ideas to enhance your Airbnb hosting experience.

Glossary of terms

Creating a glossary of terms specific to Airbnb hosting can be immensely helpful, especially for new hosts or those looking to familiarize themselves with the industry's terminology. Here's a rundown of some key terms and their meanings:

1. **Airbnb**: An online marketplace connecting people looking to rent out their homes with people looking for accommodations.

2. **Host**: The owner or manager of the listing who rents out the space to guests.

3. **Guest**: The person who books and stays at the Airbnb property.

4. **Listing**: The property is rented out on Airbnb, which includes details like location, size, price, and amenities.

5. **Superhost**: An experienced host who provides exceptional guest experiences. Airbnb awards this status based on high ratings, low cancellation rates, and the number of bookings.

6. **Instant Book**: A feature that allows guests to book a property instantly without waiting for the host's approval.

7. **Occupancy Rate**: The percentage of nights booked compared to the total available nights in a given period.

8. **Turnover**: Cleaning and preparing the property between guest stays.

9. **Check-In/Check-Out**: When guests arrive at and depart from the Airbnb property.

10.   **Short-Term Rental**: A rental period of less than six months is often used for vacation stays.

11.   **House Rules**: Guidelines set by the host for guests during their stay, covering aspects like smoking, pets, and noise levels.

12.   **Cleaning Fee**: An additional charge that covers cleaning the property after a guest's stay.

13.   **Security Deposit**: An amount held by the host for the duration of the guest's stay to cover any potential damages.

14.   **Review System**: Airbnb's feedback system where hosts and guests can review each other post-stay.

15.   **Seasonal Pricing**: Adjusting the rental price based on the season or local events to reflect demand changes.

16.   **Reservation Request**: When a guest inquires about booking a listing for specific dates before it is confirmed.

17.   **Cancellation Policy**: The terms under which guests can cancel their booking and the refunds they are eligible for.

18.   **Smart Pricing**: An Airbnb feature that automatically sets the price of a listing based on demand, time of year, and other factors.

19.   **Private Room**: A room in a shared property rented out separately.

20.   **Entire Place**: A listing where guests have the entire property.

21.   **Shared Room**: A room that guests share with others, including the host or other guests.

22.   **Experience Host**: Someone who offers unique activities or tours to guests, separate from providing accommodations.

23.   **Dynamic Pricing**: Setting flexible prices for a listing based on current market demand, competitor pricing, and other factors.

24.   **Vacation Rental**: A furnished property rented out temporarily to tourists as an alternative to a hotel.

25.   **Guest Experience**: The overall experience and satisfaction of a guest during their stay at an Airbnb.

Understanding these terms can significantly enhance your comprehension of the Airbnb platform and the short-term rental market. Whether you're a host, a guest, or someone interested in the Airbnb ecosystem, familiarity with this terminology is critical to navigating the space effectively.

DEDICATE

In closing, I would like to dedicate this book to the memory of Mark Sebring, my inspiration and mentor. Mark was not only a dear friend but also a guiding light on my journey in the world of Airbnb hosting.

Mark's passion for hospitality was infectious, and his dedication to providing exceptional guest experiences was unparalleled. His insights, wisdom, and unwavering support have left an indelible mark on me and countless others in the Airbnb community.

Mark inspired us to strive for excellence in everything we do through his generosity, kindness, and boundless enthusiasm. He believed in the power of hospitality to create connections, foster goodwill, and transform lives. His legacy lives on in the countless guests whose lives he touched and the hosts he mentored along the way.

As we bid farewell to Mark, let us honour his memory by continuing to embody the values he held dear—kindness, generosity, and a commitment to excellence. May his spirit of hospitality continue to inspire us to give our visitors experiences they will not soon forget and uphold the highest standards of service in everything we do.

Though Mark may no longer be with us in body, his presence will always be felt in the warmth of a welcome, the sincerity of a smile, and the spirit of hospitality that lives on in each of us.

Rest in peace, dear friend. Your legacy will live on in the hearts and minds of all who had the privilege of knowing you.

With heartfelt gratitude and fond memories,

Jason Westlund